Cooking Naturally

Cooking

An Evolutionary Gourmet Cuisine of Natural Foods

Naturally

by John R. Calella
Illustrations by Pedro J. Gonzalez

And/Or Press
Berkeley, California
1978

To my father, whom I love and adore, and whose support and confidence have made this book possible; and to my grandparents, who have brought great joy to my life.

Published and Distributed by
AND/OR PRESS
P.O. Box 2246
Berkeley, California 94702

ISBN: 0-915904-35-7
Library of Congress Catalog Card Number: 78-54342

Book Design by Hal Hershey
Developmental Editing by Marina LaPalma
Editing by Sayre Van Young
Typesetting by Aardvark Type
Proofreading by Intellectual Temporaries
Indexing by Sayre Van Young
Pasteup by Jane Bernard
Cover Painting by Beverly Tresan

Contents

Acknowledgements

I have had many inspired teachers and loving friends who have guided me and cared for me. My special thanks to Vincent Collura and Dr. Juan Ammon Wilkins for giving me the confidence and knowledge to be caretaker of my body. I am indebted to the works of Otto Carqué, Dr. J. H. Tilden, and Paavo Airola. They have clarified and simplified the physiological and nutritional information which has long been made complicated or unobtainable. I humbly respect the talent and genius of Herbert M. Shelton and the work he has done in making the hygienic system available to all humankind.

In the preparation of this book, Sayre Van Young's touch and her hard work have definitely added continuity. My thanks. I must gratefully acknowledge my friend Davood and his financial inspiration, and my friend Neil Hebron and his culinary inspiration; he has taught me a touch of flair. A special thank you to Janet Cross, my dearest friend. And finally, thanks to my special friend Raimondo Laudisio, master chef and a great supporter.

About the Author

Of Italian heritage, John Calella has always had a flare for cooking and a love of eating. Spaghetti, lasagna, ravioli, and breads packed the dinner tables of his early years. Though he developed a delight in the Italian cuisine, Calella eventually sensed, and his health confirmed, that the foods he was eating did not like him. He turned to an intense study of the nutritional characters of natural foods as substitutes.

First as a student of physiologist and naturopath, Dr. Juan Ammon Wilkins, and later as a student at California's Sonoma State College, Calella examined human anatomy, the biochemistry and physiology of digestion, and the art of food combining. In the course of his studies, Calella developed the Salade mandala, a picture guide to the proper combination of garden-grown foods. Calella's studies and skills have led to the formation of his natural foods catering service, his series of organic cooking classes, and the acquisition of the nickname "Organic John."

Organic John has a call-in radio show in San Francisco, and has appeared widely on radio and television with cooking demonstrations and nutritional information. A frequent lecturer on socio-nutrition, Calella has turned to Nature for the universal menu. He believes that proper nutrition can enable man to live in harmony with the environment, his fellow man, and himself. His nutritional conclusions are rooted in the theorem, "Let your food be your medicine, and your medicine your food." Paralleling Calella's growing interest in socio-nutrition has been the gradual evolvement of Organic John into the Natural Chef.

Introduction

Come with me into my kitchen. Here I daily create a sense of life for my family and friends. Here I renew my belief in the universality of Nature's Garden and the universality of the pleasures of eating.

I would like to bring you into my kitchen with this book so that you can experience the relationship between Nature's food and our gourmet pleasures. I would like to teach you how to integrate the natural into your meals and into your life. Together we can cook Old World cuisine updated to maintain the nutritional properties of the universal menu. Together we can bring New Age holistic concern to our nutritional lifestyle.

Years ago I began to develop a collection of recipes that reflected my changing feelings about what I put into my body. I observed how combinations of foods interacted with my body's chemistry and bolstered this empirical research with scientific investigations. From this evolved the concept of Salade.* This is, quite literally, salad (a dish of raw or cooked vegetables or fruits in various combinations) but with something extra. Salade emphasizes *how* foods are eaten as well as *what* foods are eaten; it stresses the combining of foods to enhance, not hinder, digestion. My recipes for complimenting courses, companion dishes, sauces, grains, and fruits are based on the chemical interactions of foods in our bodies. These combinations allow the eater to obtain the greatest nutritional benefits from the foods eaten.

As I developed my recipes, I became increasingly aware of what I call the universal menu. Many foods are available to all cultures: fruits, vegetables, grains, nuts, and seeds. Their universality became my common ground for the preparation of foods within the Salade concept. The universal menu is also the basis of the Salade mandala, a visual guide to the foods of Nature's Garden.

Before you begin cooking, study the early chapters of this book outlining the physiological concept of food combining, the importance of the acid-alkaline balance, and my preferences in food ingredients, flavor preparations, cooking methods, and utensils. I have written for both the novice cook and the sophisticated chef—for all who understand and respect food. Salade can even be combined to enrich and enhance the meal of the gourmet who dines on fish, fowl, and meats. He, too, will ask questions concerning his diet and way of life.

No matter what the level of your cooking expertise, you can embark on a Salade voyage. You need never return to an unthinking, non-nutritional way of eating—or of living—again. I firmly believe that nutrition is more than food. It is also what the Chinese call "right thinking." We can and must integrate the way we think and the way we eat with the way we live. Unless all are in harmony, we will have insufficient and inadequate nourishment for either the body or the spirit.

* Pronounced the same as salad.

Chapter One

The Meaning of Nature's Garden

"The world is so full of a number of things, I'm sure we should all be as happy as kings."
—Robert Louis Stevenson

Nature's Garden! A walk through it excites the senses and fills the body and brain with tranquility. The visual richness of the silky reds, shining greens, and glowing yellows of the fruits; the voluptousness of the vegetables, so graceful in body; the swaying of the grains as they burst from within their sheaves—here is the essence of Salade, Nature's response to man in the form of the universal menu.

According to ancient mythology, when man* started his walk in this magnificent garden, he ate the eight-petaled lotus. As his mouth became dry, he sipped from the pools of the garden. When he lay down to rest, savoring the warmth of the sun, he blinked at the brightness and realized that all the growing things in Nature's Garden needed the sun. He saw how the sun condensed the cloud vapors into rain for the pools and waterfalls, and that the water flowed to nourish the abundant and varied plant life. All life in the Garden depended on the water as well as the sun. Man began to eat from the Garden the plants nourished by the sun and the water. Satisfied, he lay back and said, "Something makes me move thorugh this Garden, and I feel strong and alive. What is this energy?"

The human body is powered by energy generated from nourishment received by plants. In simple chemical terms, the plants of Nature's Garden begin as compounds of free atoms, primarily carbon dioxide and water. Then with the energy of the sun, hundreds of atoms unite in complex molecules of potential energy: carbohydrates, proteins and fats. When man eats, and his digestive system breaks apart these molecules, their energy is liberated.

Though far removed from the lotus, we can still walk simply through this Garden. We can begin to know something of Nature and her wonders, and to know how generous she can be to those who endeavor to understand her.

Let's tour the Garden together, making sure we see all, according to Nature's plan—our Salade mandala. What better place to begin than at high noon with the artichoke, adorned with a stalk of barley. Touring clockwise through the verdure, we encounter the bamboo shoot, bean, rosemary, beet, broccoli, Brussels sprouts, buckwheat atop the white cabbage, celery, red cabbage, the rainbow-clad water chestnut, the fennel-dill family, cauliflower, Swiss chard, red Swiss chard, garbanzo beans and lentils, carrot, parsley, collard greens, corn, red and green peppers, chili peppers, thyme, millet, and the crowning parsnip. Moving on, we find the leek, scallion, eggplants purple and white, shallots, onions white and yellow, garlic with a spray of oats, kale red and green, kohlrabi and dandelion. As we come around the mandala, we find the squash clan—zucchini, butternut, Hubbard, yellow crookneck, chayote, turban, acorn, and white. Then a sheaf of rice above the okra, three varieties of

* "Man" is used here to refer to all humanity. Our language has not yet caught up with our consciousness.

cucumber, the tomato, escarole, leaf lettuce, oregano, romaine lettuce, endive, radish, daikon radish, a coronet of rye above the turnip, salsify, spinach, sweet potato, and russet, red, and new potatoes. Almost around now, we come upon the red onion, mustard greens, rutabaga with plumage of wheat, mushrooms, peas, pumpkin, watercress, basil, and asparagus.

Now our tour spirals inward into the golden realm of protein. As our path leads us again clockwise we encounter first the avocado, then the sunflower with its rich seeds, the soya bean, and the nuts—walnut, pistachio, hazel, filbert, pecan, almond, coconut cushioned by palm trees, the Brazil nut, pine or pignolia, cashew, macadamia, chestnut, then the olives green and black, peanuts, and sesame seeds.

And again inward we step gently over the beads of water into the purple province of low-acid fruits—black, red, and white star-emblazoned grapes; cactus fruit; peach nectarine; cherries of several varieties; persimmon, plums of purple, red, and green; pears; blueberries; raspberries; blackberries; huckleberries; apples; apricots; the mango; litchi nuts; papaya; guava; and cherimoya.

Clockwise again, another crossing of the beads of water into the orange order of sweet fruits—the banana; sapodillas; dates; dried cherry, pear, and peach; prunes; and raisins.

Still another bead of water crossed brings us into the magenta country of acid fruits—the tamarinds; strawberries; loganberries; kumquats; pomegranates; loquats; the glorious pineapple; gooseberries; cranberries; lime; lemon; tangerine; orange; grapefruit; and currants red, black, and green.

The final bead of water crossed finds us back among the orange-hued sweet fruits, including the dried fruits—currants, pineapple, apricots; and figs; fresh figs too, breadfruit; and carob.

An aureole of water beads highlights the melons—cantaloupes, Persian (casaba), honeydew, and watermelon—interspersed with flowers signifying the moon's aspects: new, waxing, full, and waning. Then the seven waterfalls embracing the rainbow-colored lotus with the cloud-cradled sun as the nucleus of all life. Our tour of the Salade mandala has been inward; it is time to gaze outward where we see the Garden completed by the four seasons: winter, spring, summer, and fall.

The Meaning of Salade

Salade is an intelligence of all things in Nature's Garden, delicately blended and seasoned with natural minerals and herbs. Salade is the ideal way of combining foods and enhancing the senses. It recommends that seasonings and dressings do not predominate, that food is chopped well and allowed to dance in the mouth, and that all food is eaten with respect.

Salade is an involvement with Nature. It's a way of examining the inherent wisdom of plant life so that we can best utilize that wisdom for the chemical intelligence of our bodies. We must learn to ask, "How do I take from the environment what will give me the maximum health? How do I combine myself with the things inherent in Nature so that I may grow, and interact with all living things with knowledge?"

Salade is also harmony. With a humane and compassionate use of our technology and science we can make an environment where no scarcity exists. But we must learn about nourishing the internal environment. Taking a walk in nature is not enough. It is important to walk inwardly with Nature, to let Nature flow through our veins so that we may participate in the growing relationship with all living things.

Salade is discipline. I believe that man pollutes his outside environment because he pollutes himself inwardly. Fat, that internal waste which blows up and distorts the human organism—the same waste that can result in malnutrition—occurs because we do not feed ourselves properly. Salade's only restrictions are the controls built into the environment. We cannot just throw into our bodies whatever we think they may like.

Salade is flexibility. We must interact with the environment as does the bamboo: if it is not flexible, it will break with the first strong wind. Delightful, sensuous flexibility allows us to assimilate, digest, and enjoy the foods in Nature's Garden.

Salade emphasizes inquiry into food combinations. The idea of combining foods into salads or stews or soups has been with us for centuries. It is thought that when man became bored with single foods, he mixed one or more together, for better or worse. If the latter, he invented disguises: thick sauces, immoderate spices, heavy dressings. Salade combines foods thoughtfully, for enhancement of delicate tastes, for nutritional benefits, and for digestive ease.

Salade involves a dialogue with our food. We often talk about what foods we like, but seldom do we ask, "Do the things we like, like us?" If we fail to seek the reasons why we select the things we eat, we cannot understand the alternatives available for inner contentment and robust health.

I'll show you that you can eat things you like and like the things you eat. They are delicious and nutritious, an unbeatable combination. We will go beyond eating as an immoderate fetish, as an inflexible, compulsive act, so that we may eat rays of the sun and feast upon the seasons, so that *we* can be winter, spring, summer, and autumn.

The Salade mandala is a graphic illustration of my nutritional approach to life. But food is only one of the materials in the grand physiological process of nutrition. Food and its seven basic nutrients (vitamins, minerals, proteins, carbohydrates, essential fatty acids, enzymes, and trace elements) have value in concert with the other elements that constitute optimal nutrition. It is on these ten bars of nutrition that we can all play a symphony of life:

Sunshine: the energy-producing force for all life.
Pure water: Nature's elixir of life.
Pure air: a breath of freshness.
Exercise: rhythmic movement in Nature's playground.
Rest and Relaxation: quiet time with your heart.
Love of life and tranquil thoughts: inner peace.
Real foods: in proper combination.
Bio-synthetic foods: the combination of the laboratory and the garden.
People: a source of energy.
Humane use of technology: an end to routine and drudgery, with more access to choices.

Chapter Two

Classifying the Garden

"Our bodies are our gardens, to the which our wills are gardeners."

—William Shakespeare

To appreciate Salade and the universal menu we must understand the foods in Nature's Garden and their relationships to each other and to man. I've presented my simplified scheme here, classifying foods into groups of food high in sugars, starches, fats, proteins, and organic minerals. We will also look more closely at the fruits and vegetables, the cornerstones of the Salade concept. Definitions and discussion of alkaline and acid will follow, with a listing of those foods forming each. All this will help give you a better idea of the chemical composition and effects of various foods. But don't lose sight (or taste!) of Nature as food poet, not just as food chemist. Nature does not turn out proteins, but pecans, avocados, beans; not carbohydrates, but potatoes, rutabagas, carrots; not minerals, but greens and fruits; not sugars, but dates, figs, pineapples.

The Food Groups

Group I: Sugars

Foods high in sugar—sweet carbohydrates—are easily digested and readily assimilated. They offer the body quick heat and energy and help to maintain its normal temperature.

The predominant elements in natural sugars are carbon, hydrogen, and oxygen, with traces of iron and other minerals.

The natural sugars are:

beet sugar and syrup
cane sugar and syrup
honey
maple sugar and syrup
syrup from sweet fruits

Foods high in sugar are:

carob
dates
figs
grapes
persimmons
pineapples
prunes
raisins
sorghum
sugar beets
sugar cane
sweet berries
watermelons

Group II: Starches

Starches, when masticated well and digested, are converted into sugars and used as fuel for heating the body and giving energy. Starches should be eaten sparingly as it is all too easy to develop a starch addiction, causing the pancreas to overwork. They are best combined with a green salad, due to their digestive compatability; bananas, however, should be eaten alone or with other sweet fruits.

As with those foods in Group I, the elements in starchy foods are carbon, hydrogen, and oxygen; starches are also known as carbohydrates.

Starchy foods include:

bananas
beans (all kinds)
grains and grain products
  (rice, rye, wheat, etc.)
parsnips
potatoes (Irish and sweet)
pumpkin
squash (Hubbard and
  banana)

Group III: Fats

These highly concentrated foods are not easily digested, but when oxidized they produce heat and energy for the body. The main elements in fats are also carbon, hydrogen, and oxygen, with carbon predominating. Fats are chemically classed as hydrocarbons.

Fats are predominant in:

avocados
butter
cheese (not cottage)
coconuts
cream
margarine
mayonnaise
nuts
oils (100% fat)
peanut butter

Group IV: Proteins

Proteins provide the body with the necessary materials for the building and replacing of cells and tissues. They also produce heat and energy for the body. The basic elements found in all proteins are nitrogen, carbon, hydrogen, and oxygen. Some proteins also contain sulphur, phosporus, and small amounts of other minerals. As proteins contain a good deal of nitrogen they are chemically known as nitrogenous foods.

We have been led to believe that we are not getting enough protein in our diet, mainly because the suggested level of protein intake was so outrageously high—some nutritionists advocated an intake of as much as 120 grams of protein a day. More recently, however, nutritionists have been re-examining man's protein needs and have revised downward their estimates—many now suggest no more than 50 grams a day, with some even setting 25 grams as a reasonable limit.

Let me share with you some of my investigations and feelings about protein. Essentially, I feel that man does not utilize more than 25 grams of protein a day; I feel that the body does not need a constant supply of protein, even though the body utilizes protein on a daily basis; and finally, that the over-emphasis on proteins is misplaced. On observing myself, my father, and my friends when fasting, I've discovered little if any drop in protein level, as measured by tests of serum albumin, even with lengthy fasts during which water is ingested.

Proteins are part of the nutritional process, not the whole story. Do not be deceived into thinking that because something is good for you, a lot of it is better. Balance and harmony are the keys.

In determining the amount of protein you require, consider such factors as the type of work you do, your body size and build, whether you are extremely active or less so, the demands of the weather, and the level of stress you daily encounter. For the person who is average in all of these, a diet of fruits, green vegetables, nuts, seeds, sprouts, and grains (with the possible addition of raw egg yolks) will maintain the body's well-being.

Protein foods include:

avocados
beans (all kinds)
cheese (all kinds)
eggs
fish
fowl
grains (glutenous portion)
lentils
meat
mushrooms
nuts (all kinds; also rich in fats)
olives
peas (all kinds)
seeds (all kinds)
soya beans

Group V: Organic Minerals

If there is a keystone to the universal menu of Nature's Garden, it is the organic minerals. They are vital for maintaining body's chemistry. The alkaline minerals—iron, calcium, potassium, magnesium, fluorine, iodine, silicon, and sodium—are instrumental in building the body's tissues into a formidible barrier to combat a host of diseases. Foods rich in the alkaline minerals should constitute three-quarters of your menu, with foods from the other four food groups making up the remaining quarter.

These foods are rich in the organic alkaline minerals vital to normal body chemistry:

apples
apricots
artichokes (French)
beets (roots and greens)
blueberries
broccoli
Brussels sprouts
buttermilk
cabbage
cauliflower

carrots
celery
chard
cherries
cranberries
cucumbers
dandelion greens
eggplants
endive
garlic
gooseberries
grapes
grapefruits
huckleberries
kale
kohlrabi
leeks
lemons
lettuce
mustard greens
oranges
parsley
parsnips
peaches
pears
peas
peppers (green)
pineapples
plums
pomegranates
prunes
radishes
raspberries
savoy cabbage
spinach
squash (summer)
strawberries
string beans
tangerines
tomatoes
turnip greens
watercress
youngberries

Fruits

A fruit (from the Latin *fructus*, meaning enjoyment) is the mature ovary of a flowering plant with its contents and it's closely connected parts. To me, fruits are simply Nature's storage batteries. They have particular value as internal cleaners of the body; and they're also packed with vitamins and minerals. I group fruits according to their chemical composition, as acid, low-acid, and sweet, but all are alkaline-forming foods in the body (except for prunes and plums). All are charged with the electrical energy of sunlight; their nutritive value is solar power.

This classification includes raw fruits in their natural states. For digestive compatibility, it is best to eat no more than three fruits at the same meal and preferably from the same class.

Acid fruits are:

cranberries
currants
gooseberries
grapefruits
kumquats
lemons
limes
loganberries
loquats
oranges
pineapples
pomegranates
strawberries
sour apples
tangerines
tamarinds
tree or cherry tomatoes

Low-acid fruits are:

apples
apricots
avocados
blackberries
blueberries
cactus fruits
cherimoyas
cherries
elderberries
fujoas
grapes
guavas
huckleberries
litchi nuts
mangos
mulberries
nectarines
papayas
pawpaws
peaches
pears
persimmons
plums
quinces
raspberries
soursops

Sweet fruits are:

bananas
breadfruits
carob
dates
dried fruits (all types)
figs
jackfruits
prunes
raisins
sapodillas
sapotes

Vegetables

The fantastic mineral qualities in vegetables mark them as vital foods in the human diet. Their nutritional benefits will be squandered unless care is taken in their preparation, however. Vegetables can be prepared without greatly altering their chemical composition if not cooked to death. Anything heated to 130° or over for more than fifteen minutes should be considered dead as all the enzymes have been destroyed. When steaming vegetables, be sure to drink the residue liquid; it contains an assortment of minerals. The combination of vegatables need not be as strict as with fruits.

Non-starchy vegetables are:

anise
artichokes
asparagus
basil
beans (green)
beet greens
borage
broccoli
Brussels sprouts
cabbage
caraway
catnip
cauliflower
celeriac
celery
chard
chervil
chicory
chives
collard greens
corn (young, fresh)
cucumbers
dandelion greens
eggplants
endives
fennel
garden cress
garlic
kale
kohlrabi
leeks
lettuce
mushrooms
mustard greens
okra
onions
parsley
peas
peppers
radishes
rocket
sage
sea kale
sorrel
spinach
squash (young)
thyme
tomatoes
turnips
watercress

Slightly starchy vegetables are:

beets
burdock
carrots
parsnips
rutabagas
salsify

Starchy vegetables are:

barley
beans (dried)
buckwheat
chestnuts
corn (mature)
millet
oats
peanuts
peas (dried)
potatoes (all types)
pumpkin
rice
rye
squash(Hubbard)
wheat

Acid and Alkaline

Acid and alkaline are terms used to describe the chemistry of the body's metabolism. It is best to have a diet rich in the alkaline-forming foods—the superalkaline foods—thus maintaining a high state of alkalinity in the body. The more alkaline the blood, the freer the body from disease. The body's oxidation of foods ingested results in the formation of an ash or residue. If the predominant minerals in the food eaten are sodium, potassium, calcium, or magnesium, the result is an alkaline ash. If the predominant minerals in the foods eaten are sulfur, phosphorus, or chlorine, the result is an acid ash. The nature and proportions of these oxidation ashes determine the acid-alkaline balance in the bloodstream.

I feel the most appropriate balance of acidity-alkalinity is a one to three ratio. That is eat one food high in acid minerals to three foods high in alkaline minerals. Naturally, your physician can best determine your exact acid-alkaline balance.

I would like to point out a good way to deal with acidosis, a condition in which the body's alkali reserve falls below normal. It is often suggested in this case that one eliminate fruits from the diet. When the body is very acid, the alkaline properties of the fruits have an immediate effect on neutralizing the acidic condition in the blood. However, the sudden and startling effect the fruits have on the condition is often made the culprit of the distress! Rather than forever eliminating fruits, I feel it is best to detoxify the body through a cleansing and fasting regime and then to slowly reintroduce the vital and health-giving fruits. Two particularly good sources of information on this and the acid-alkaline question in general are Juan Ammon Wilkins' book *Coconuts and Constipation* and Dr. Herbert Shelton's study, *Superior Nutrition.*

Acid-forming foods include:

acorns
animal byproducts
artichokes (Jerusalem)
asparagus tips
barley
beans (dried)
beechnuts
Brazil nuts
buckwheat
chestnuts
coconuts
corn (mature, dried)
dairy products (all types, except raw milk)
eggs
fish (all types)
grains (all types)
hickory nuts
honey
lentils
legumes
macadamia nuts
margarines (animal and vegetable)
meat (all types)
meat extracts
millet
oats
peanuts
pecans
pistachio nuts
plums
prunes
rhubarb
rice
rye
shellfish (all types)
walnuts
wheat

all starches, e.g., macaroni and spaghetti
all sugars, e.g., white, brown, honey
all nuts (with the exception of almonds, butter-nuts, cashews, and hazelnuts)
all improperly combined foods
all overly cooked foods
all highly seasoned foods
all canned and preserved foods
all TV dinners

Alkaline-forming foods include:

almonds
anise
apples
apricots
artichokes (French)
asparagus (stems)
avocados
bananas
basil
beans (fresh)
beets
blackberries
breadfruits
broccoli
Brussels sprouts
butternuts
caraway
carob
carrots
cashews
catnip
cauliflower
celeriac
celery
chard
cherimoya
cherries
chervil
chicory
chives
collard greens
corn (young only)
cranberries
cress
cucumbers
currants
dandelion greens
dates
eggplants
elderberries
endives
fennel
figs
garlic
gooseberries
grapefruits
grapes
guavas
hazelnuts
huckleberries
jackfruits
kale
kohlrabi
leeks
lemons
lettuce (all types)
lima beans
limes
loquats
mangos
melons (all types)
milk (raw only)
mulberries
mushrooms
mustard greens
nectarines
okra
olives
onions
oranges
papayas
parsley
parsnips
pawpaws
peaches
pears
peas
peppers
persimmons
pineapples
pomegranates
potatoes (not fried)
pumpkin
quinces
radishes
raisins
raspberries
rocket
rutabagas
salsify
sauerkraut (when not cooked or pickled)
sapotes
sea kale
seeds (all types)
sorrel
soursop
spinach
squash
strawberries
sweet potatoes
tamarinds
tangerines
tomatoes
tree or cherry tomatoes
turnips

Chapter Three

Digestion and Food Combining

"There are no health foods, per se, only foods that are properly combined."

—Organic John, the Natural Chef

Digestion

To understand the precepts of food combining, we must first consider the process of digestion. Simply, digestion is the changing of food into a form that the body can use. No matter how long you hold an apple to your forehead, its nutritional possibilities wil remain unrealized by your body. But eat that apple—expose it to the digestive juices of your mouth, stomach, and intestines—and the energy of the apple will become yours.

The juices capable of such a transformation contain enzymes, or physiological catalysts, each of which acts upon a specific substance at a specific point in the digestive tract. The enzyme pepsin, for example, aids in the digestion of proteins in the stomach; ptyalin aids in the conversion in the mouth and throat of starch into the sugar maltose, and so on. Proper digestion involves the proper timing of enzyme secretions, that is, the *rates* at which different enzymes are secreted upon different foods, and the *order* in which different enzymes act upon a food in the complete breakdown of the food into a form that can be utilized or stored by the body.

It is the eater's task to provide a postitive physical atmosphere for digestion. It is inappropriate to the harmony and moderation of the Salade concept to eat a hectic lunch at your desk during business hours, or to eat what the kids left on their plates as you clean up after a meal. Remember these rules for gentleness to your digestion:

1) Do not eat when tired or exhausted.
2) Do not eat under stress.
3) Do not eat when sick. Allow your body to free itself from the dis-eased condition before you confuse it with digestive demands on your limited body strength.
4) Do not drink liquids at the same time you are eating. They dilute or float the enzymes, interfering with salivary and gastric digestion.
5) Eat only when hungry. This seems the most obvious of dietary and digestive maxims, but it is also the most neglected.
6) Eat in a peaceful and tranquil atmosphere.

Food Combining

I've mentioned food combining as we walked through Nature's Garden. I'd like to explain in detail what it is and how proper food combinations are part of the Salade concept. In this context, it may be helpful to refer to the Salade mandala, our picture guide to the proper combination of garden-grown foods.

Although Nature's Garden provides our universal menu, it is our task to select appropriate food combinations. I don't mean combining foods as we have been taught to in the typical American meal: soup, salad, main dish, bread, dessert, beverage. I combine foods not by their culinary nature, but by their nutritional and chemical natures. Food combining is a way to provide our bodies, at each meal, with the foods that it can best utilize. Our digestive systems are not designed to handle conflicting foods. Each digestive enzyme acts upon a specific substance at a specific time and place in the digestive process; many of the enzymes, if simultaneously activated, will cancel out each other, resulting in poor digestion of certain foods and inadequate utilization of their nutrients by the body.

The ideal meal begins with those foods containing the greatest amounts of liquid, such as green, leafy, raw vegetables, and continues with complementing courses of cooked vegetables and delicate companion dishes. Fruits are to be considered as meals unto themselves, and not as desserts. And as each food contains its own juices and liquids, the consumption of beverages during the meal is not necessary.

If you wish to consume proteins at your meal, it is vital to consider their digestive compatabilities, not only of proteins with starches, fats, or sugars, but of one kind of protein with another. Proteins of diverse origins—meat, milk, eggs, beans—require different digestive time schedules. The strength and rate of flow of the juices secreted by digestive organs differes with these various sources of protein. For example, the flesh foods (meat, fish, fowl) receive the strongest digestive secretions during the first hour of digestion; milk receives the strongest secretions at the end of the digestive process; and eggs and beans receive the strongest secretions at still other points in the digestive process. Therefore, I suggest no more than one conentrated protein be eaten at each meal.

The combination of proteins with starches (cereals, breads, rice) is digestively disasterous. Starches require an alkaline medium in the mouth while proteins undergo digestion in an acid medium. In turn, the digestive enzymes secreted in the stomach are unable to deal with both proteins and starches at the same time, as protein digestion involves the secretion of hydrochloric acid, creating an acid environment highly inhibitive to the digestion of starches. I strongly suggest that protein and starchy foods be eaten at separate meals.

What about proteins and fats—gravy or butter with meats, for example? The fats may inhibit the secretion of gastric juices for up to two hours, with an obvious deleterious effect on digestion. Therefore, *I suggest that fats and proteins be eaten at separate meals.*

Proteins and sugars (honey, syrups, dates, bananas, etc.) are also an unsatisfactory food combination. All sugars inhibit the secretion of gastric juices; they are digested in the intestine and are not held long in the stomach when taken alone. This is one reason for the quick energy sugars can provide the body. But when combined with proteins, the sugars tend to ferment as they cannot pass into the intestine until the proteins have been digested in the stomach. *I suggest that sugars and proteins be eaten at separate meals.*

Let's look at one more protein combination, that of proteins with acid foods, such as the acid fruits. Protein digestion begins with pepsin, and it is this very enzyme that is inhibited by the acids from fruits. *I suggest that acid foods and proteins be eaten at separate meals.* An exception is cheese and nuts; these protein foods are high in fats, and fats and acid foods combine well.

Seeds are a unique protein food, rich in many healthful nutrients and highly concentrated. Because of their high concentration (in nutrients as well as oils, vitamin E, and unsaturated fatty acids) they should be eaten consistently, but in small quantities. Their nutritional value is not duplicated anywhere, in Nature's Garden or man's laboratories. Remember to masticate well, as poorly chewed seeds can cause digestive upsets. A blender or nutgrinder is useful here. As with other protein foods, seeds should also be carefully combined to enhance, not cripple, digestion. Seeds are alkaline-forming unlike animal and nut proteins (with a few exceptions). They're best with vegetables, either raw or cooked, and should not be combined with starches. Soaked, sprouted seeds are best combined with green, leafy vegetables.

Eggs are really seeds, each containing a life-support system for the future. The yolk is composed of fat, protein, and minerals; it is best eaten separately from the white and preferably raw. If you choose the whole egg, boil or poach it. Eggs, like seeds, are highly concentrated foods and must be eaten wisely. Follow the rules of protein combination for best digestion.

Food combining also involves the proper combination of liquids with the more solid portions of meals. As mentioned earlier, our ideal meal begins with the foods containing the greatest amount of natural liquid (as opposed to an added sauce or broth); as each food has its own juices, there is no need for drinking a beverage at the meal. You can and should drink, before the meal, the residue liquid from the meal's vegetables. This is rich in minerals, and by drinking it before eating, you will not upset the digestive process. Drinking fluids with a meal will dilute the digestive enzymes and interfere with salivary and gastric digestion. If thirsty, drink liquids at least fifteen minutes before eating. When having a raw salad, be it fruit or vegetable, wait forty-five minutes after eating before consuming liquids. When having cooked vegetables that are non-starchy or slightly starchy, wait at least an hour after eating to drink liquids. When having cooked starchy vegetables or starch such as bread or macaroni, wait at least two hours after eating to drink liquids. When having proteins, wait at least four hours after eating to drink liquids. Remember, *beverages should be consumed separately from meals.*

Because of its combined fat protein content, milk combines poorly with almost all foods. I always consider it a meal, and not a beverage. *I suggest that milk be consumed alone or with acid fruits.*

We've already examined starches in concert with proteins, but what about the combination of starchy food and such acid foods as oranges, lemons, grapefruits, vinegar, tomatoes, etc.? Ptyalin, a starch-splitting enzyme, can act only in an alkaline medium. Yet acid foods contain oxalic acid, a tiny portion of which is sufficient to arrest the action of ptyalin on starches. *I suggest starches and acid foods be eaten at separate meals.*

Do not mix two starches at the same meal, nor even a slightly starchy vegetable with a starchy vegetable. This contributes to overconsumption of starches, a viscious cycle. If you do any starch combining, always include some green, leafy vegetables. *I suggest no more than one starch be eaten at each meal.*

Starches with sugars are also inappropriate at best, and indigestible at worst. When sugar is present in the mouth, the saliva contains no ptyalin; since starch digestion begins in the mouth with the action of ptyalin, the effect of sugar on the saliva inhibits starch digestion in the mouth. In turn, the digestion of sugar cannot take place until starch digestion is completed in the stomach. *I suggest eating starches and sugars at separate meals.*

Fruits, like most foods in Nature's Garden, can best be eaten with other foods of the same class: acid fruits with acid fruits, low-acid fruits with low-acid fruits, and sweet fruits with other sweet fruits. Fair combinations are acid fruits with the green, leafy lettuces or with low-acid fruits. Create interesting variety by combining the acid fruits with proteins, or the low-acid fruits with the sweet ones. However, *I suggest that as much as possible, you eat fruits by themselves.*

Melons (watermelon, cantaloupe, honeydew) are

digested in the intestines as are other fruits. When eaten with foods that are digested in the stomach, digestion is delayed; fermentation can occur in the stomach since the melon cannot pass into the intestines until the accompanying foods are digested in the stomach. *I suggest that melons always be eaten alone.*

Desserts in general—cakes, custards, pies, puddings, ice cream, stewed fruits, and the myriad over-processed sweetnesses available in the supermarket—serve no useful purpose digestively or nutritionally. If you must consume them, at least do your body a favor and eat them with a raw green salad. *I suggest, however, that you desert the desserts.*

Rules for Optimal Food Combination

1) Eat like foods together.
2) Eat no more than one concentrated protein at each meal.
3) Eat starches and proteins at separate meals.*
4) Eat fats and proteins at separate meals.
5) Eat sugars and proteins at separate meals.
6) Eat acids and proteins at separate meals.
7) Do not consume beverages during the meal.*
8) Drink milk alone or with acid fruits.
9) Eat starches and acid foods at separate meals.
10) Eat no more than one starch at each meal.
11) Eat starches and sugars at separate meals.
12) Eat fruits alone, especially melons.
13) Desert the desserts.

* These rules are of particular importance.

Chapter Four

Eating Naturally: Ingredients, Preparation, Cooking, Serving

Eating would certainly be easier—but oh so boring—if we ate only one food throughout our lives, or several foods prepared in only one way. The myriad delights of Nature's Garden can be enhanced by variety of food, seasoning, preparation, cooking, and serving; it is each of these I'd like to talk about now.

Ingredients

All the foods used in this book are fresh. Nothing is canned or preserved; nothing contains chemicals or artificial coloring. The only ingredients that come in glass are tamari sauce, pure vegetable extracts, mineral and protein powders, mineral bouillons, olives, and oils.

Shopping for high quality, fresh produce can be quite a hassle, especially outside of California. Find a small market with sufficient turnover where the produce looks garden fresh and the owner takes pride in offering high quality and variety at realistic prices. If possible, grow your own or become part of a community gardening plan. Produce that has been allowed to ripen almost to full maturity will have the best flavor and highest nutritional content.

Some of the ingredients for a particular recipe may be out of season. If a certain green cannot be found, for example, substitute another of your choice. Experiment! In only one instance, however, would I recommend the substitution of frozen for fresh vegetables, and that is with green peas (though do thaw them before use). Try not to buy more fresh produce than you can use in twelve hours. You will shop more often, but you will eat more naturally.

The salting and peppering of foods in this country seems a preconceived ceremony. Natural flavors are diffused in favor of the camouflaging effects of irritating sodium chloride and pepper. Doctors and nutritionists continue arguing the pros and cons of salt in the diet, and the battle is best left to them; the seasonings used in this book are minerals, savories, and herbs—all in their natural forms. Except for flavor preparations, all seasonings should be fresh, if possible. If you use commercial seasoning, vary proportions to your own taste.

My preference in cooking and salad oils is nearly always olive oil. However, there are many other excellent oils, such as safflower, sesame, or peanut oils. Use your own flavor choice, providing the oil is cold pressed, that is, has been extracted with a hydraulic press without heat, and is unrefined.

Soya and safflower butters, unsalted and without artificial coloring, are often called for in my recipes; like other butters, they come in quarter-pound cubes. Although partially hydrogenated, these butters don't have the negative effects of hydrogenated fat foods. Do

not use these in cooking; rather, add to already cooked food, allow to melt, and stir in before serving. If you cannot locate either soya or safflower butter, you may substitute raw milk butter, unsalted and without artificial coloring.

The Salade concept is universal as Nature's Garden is worldwide. Nevertheless, certain man-made ingredients—syrups, powders, seasonings—are less widespread, and will need to be purchased in natural food, ethnic, or speciality stores. They are recommended for their purity and taste-enhancing qualities, they are all well worth seeking out. For your convenience, I have listed these flavor preparations, and what they contain.

Mineral bouillon is an all-vegetable liquid concentrate made from whole wheat; corn; cane; lemon, orange, and papaya juice solids; soya lecithin; and ocean dulse. This soya amino acid protein is mineralized with balanced potassium, calcium, phosphorus, iron, and magnesium chloride mineral salts. It is added to food in its concentrated form.

Mineral powder (broth) is a dry powder prepared from uncooked green celery, tomatoes, spinach, red bell peppers, parsley, watercress, sesame seeds, and sea kelp, flavored with yeast, orange aromatic herbs, and vegetable seasoning. Sold in powder form, it can be used to make a broth; hence you'll often find both terms on the label. I particularly like Dr. Jensen's Mineral Broth Seasoning.

Miso is essentially a seasoning purée, prepared from the aged fermented culture of cooked soybeans, salt, and water. It's high in lactobacillus acidophilus and protein. Miso doesn't need to be refrigerated until opened.

Tamari, or Japanese soya sauce, is a seasoning liquid prepared from fermented soya beans, salt, water, and wheat, aged from eighteen to twenty-four months. It doesn't have the nutritional value of other products listed here, and I have included it only as a commonly-used non-chemical, taste-enhancing substance. It's use is a matter of personal preference. Because of tamari's high sodium content, I avoid it completely and substitute mineral bouillon instead.

Carrot syrup comes from organically-grown carrots reduced to a syrup by the low temperature, high vacuum cooking method. Trace minerals in carrot syrup include calcium, iron, and potassium, and vitamins A, C, and D.

Kelp is dried and granulated sea kelp, processed under exacting conditions for purity. The brand I prefer is Par Kelp, a Norwegian product.

Instant protein powder contains soya protein concentrate, fructose, lecithin, calcium carbonate, yeast, potassium chloride, and natural flavors. Loaded with vitamins and minerals, it can be used as a drink mix, or to add flavor to all salads, fruit and nut sherberts, fruit drinks, and cooked vegetables. This excellent food supplement can also be freely used by hypoglycemics and diabetics with no negative effects as it contains fructose, rather than dextrose. I prefer Shaklee's Instant Protein.

Lecithin granules aid the liver in the digestion of fats. Best natural sources of lecithin include soya beans, egg yolks, cold-pressed unrefined olive oil, and some cheese products. In granular form, available at health food stores, lecithin is best with vegetables.

Soyamel powder made from dried soya beans, is high in protein and lecithin. It is best with fruit sherberts and creams. Soyamel powder and liquid soya milk are not the same, though their relationship is the same as powdered cow's milk and liquid milk.

Sesame tahini, ground hulled sesame nuts, has a rich nutty taste. It contains no preservatives and needs no refrigeration. Use it as a nut butter; it's especially delicious with tomatoes.

Balanced protein seasoning is a hydrolyzed vegetable protein, in powder form, made from unrefined soya beans. It contains no stabilizers or animal products.

Yeast is a delightful food, adding flavor to salad dressings, cooked vegetables, and starchy dishes. It is especially delicious sprinkled on spaghetti, replacing cheese. Yeast contains a rich supply of protein, vitamins, and minerals. I use NB500 Brewers' Organic Yeast Flakes as sold by Life Force or Dr. Donsbach's Nutritional Yeast. Throughout the recipes here I will refer simply to nutritional yeast.

SeaZun is an all-purpose seasoning, a blend from the sea and the garden: sea kelp, celery seeds, onions, paprika, thyme, garlic, chili powder, cardamom, sweet basil, and bay leaves. This powder blend is an excellent way of adding vitamins and minerals to your salads and cooked foods while enriching flavor.

Dulse powder is simply powdered sea lettuce; it provides added minerals and has no unpleasant fishy taste. I particularly like it on tomatoes and onions or in green leafy salads.

Ginger powder is more than a spice. Coming from the ginger root, its medicinal and health properties have no counterpart in our Garden. I prefer the root fresh, but the use of the powder when fresh ginger is unavailable adds both flavor and nutrition to your cooking.

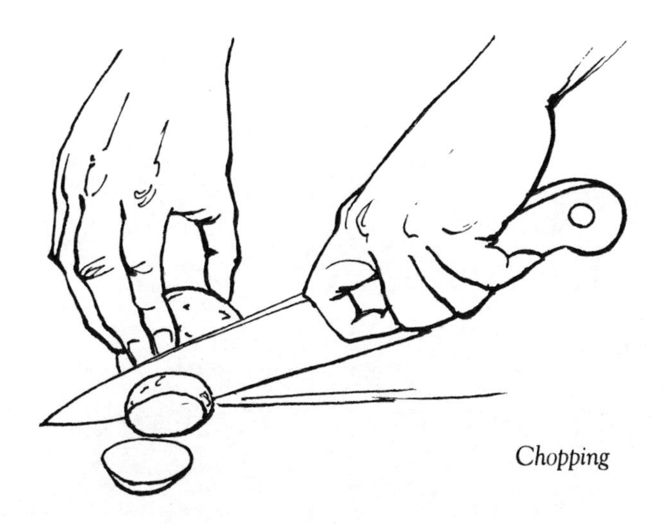
Chopping

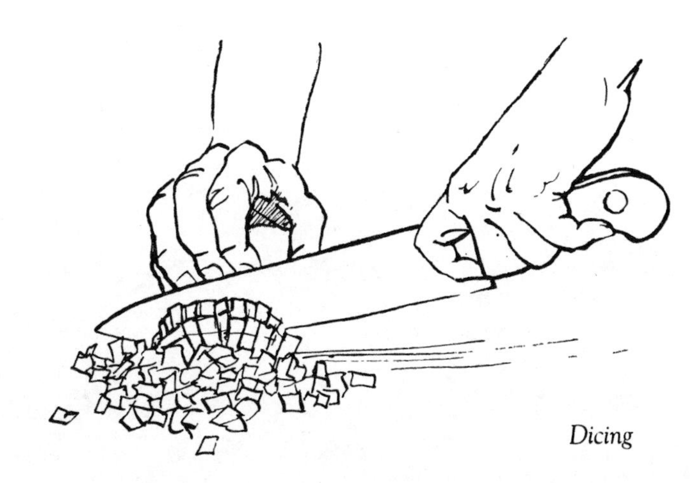
Dicing

Preparation

The proper mastication of foods is vital to your health and to your enjoyment of foods. Large, thick morsels are difficult to chew and digest, and do not allow delicate natural food flavors to be savored. Foods that are chopped, sliced, and diced with precision and uniformity can be enjoyed more fully, while aiding in the digestion process. Use of the basic cutting and slicing techniques will allow you to present foods in all their natural splendor.

Needless to say, it is important to have a sharp cutting utensil appropriate to the job: chopper, chopping knife, paring knife, peeler, etc. Esssential also is a stable smooth work surface—no chopping on the kitchen sink drainboard. Invest in a large wooden chopping board—it'll last a lifetime.

These are the basic food preparations methods that I find myself using over and over. In my recipes I indicate specific procedures to prepare foods, but as with many of my suggestions, use them as guides, not as laws. If you want to slice something that I suggest should be cubed, go ahead and try it. There is always room for experimentation and inspiration in the Salade concept.

Peeling is the removal of the outer covering or skin of a food. I have a general rule about peeling: avoid where possible. I indicate only if it's integral part of preparation for a particular recipe. But use your discretion throughout; many people are unable to digest the skins of eggplant or cucumber, for example. I'd rather you peel eggplant and cucumbers than not eat them (and always peel if they have waxy coats or are from non-organic plants). However, never peel and discard potato skins—hidden in those skins is a nutritional bonanza. Besides, they taste good.

Chopping is the process of separating foods into many pieces with a sharp knife. It's best when preparing vegetables for purées and stuffings, or as a preliminary step in mixing vegetables.

Cubing is cutting food into small squares about an inch square.

Dicing is cutting foods into even smaller squares, like dice. Both cubing and dicing are useful techniques for preparing chunky pieces that will maintain their shape.

Slicing is the process of making repeated solid strokes with a knife to form slender pieces. I often slice foods in the Oriental fashion, that is, in long slender pointed pieces of a similar size that will stir-fry quickly and evenly.

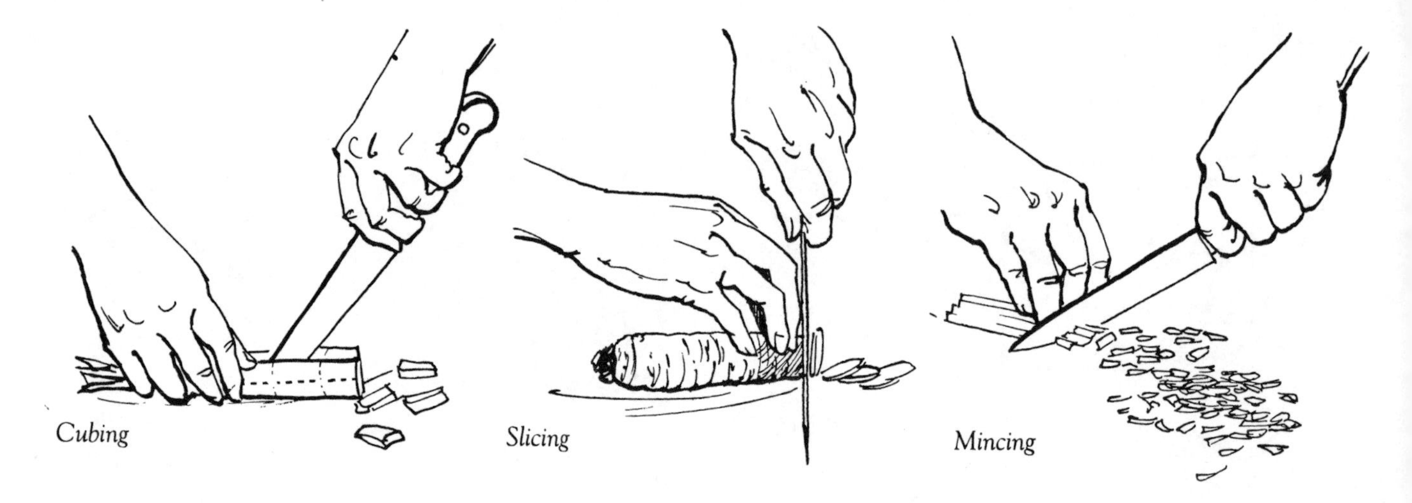
Cubing *Slicing* *Mincing*

Mincing is cutting foods into very small pieces; I usually mince garlic or parsley, for example.

Shredding is to tear or cut foods into long narrow pieces. Cabbage is a food that is often shredded.

Coring is often used for preparation of fruits, such as coring an apple or pear. This process of removing the middle of a food can also be employed when making stuffed cabbages, for example; just don't core all the way to the bottom. I consider it more of a scooping method when applied to vegetables.

Hand-squeezing is a tactile way to deal with tomatoes. Simply squeeze the tomato, letting the pulp and seeds fall into your dish or pan, then drop the outer shell in too. It's a very satisfying technique!

And then there are all the miscellaneous methods: quartering, halving, the making of melon balls, and other self-explanatory processes.

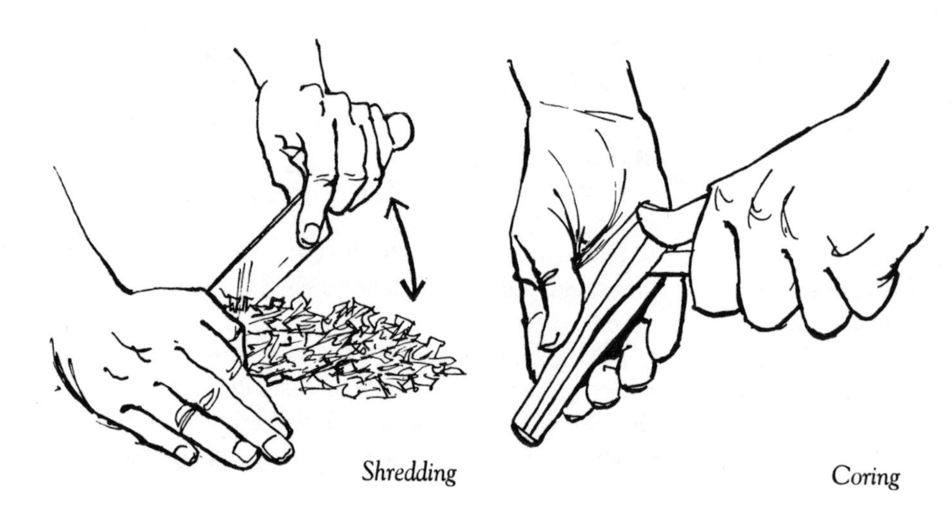
Shredding *Coring*

Cooking Utensils

Throughout the recipes that follow, you will find yourself repeatedly using the same utensils: my basic array of tools. These will include a chopping board and knife, a covered roasting pan, skillets for sautéing, covered pans for steaming, a steamer or collander for use inside the covered pan, a wok and wok utensils, small bowls for mixing stocks, and a collection of wooden spoons, forks, etc.

Beware of the many pitfalls in selecting cooking utensils. Most culinary shops pander to the whims of the collector and decorator first, and only secondarily to the needs of the cook. Cooking utensils, like cooking and eating, offer a personal involvement. All the implements I use and recommend have been selected because they are functional, durable, and psychologically pleasing to me.

I prefer porcelain-clad **pots and pans** for low flame cooking, and copper and steel utensils for intense heats, such as sautéing. There is a theory that the aluminum in cookware can react negatively with the juices in some foods. To me, aluminum pots and pans impart a metallic taste to fruits and vegetables, discolor many foods, and give them a dried and unappetizing appearance. I don't recommend their use for cooking or serving. Nor do I use iron pans. Some suggest that the iron of the pan bleeds into the food, adding nourishment. However, this iron is not chelated, resulting in the discoloration of food, especially acid foods, and the physiological problems resulting from non-chelated iron. I won't even discuss Teflon.

Be sure to wash pots and pans immediately after use; I try to wash all my cooking utensils before I sit down to eat. If pots and pans are left to sit, they develop a scrub-resistant film which absorbs the acidity of the cooked foods; this interferes with cooking on a practical level, and more importantly, can be a health hazard as bacteria can be absorbed by the film. If you do use iron pans, be sure to clean and store them properly. Wash immediately after

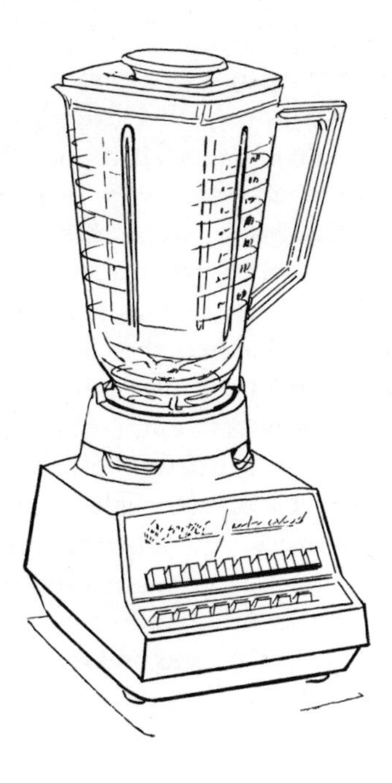

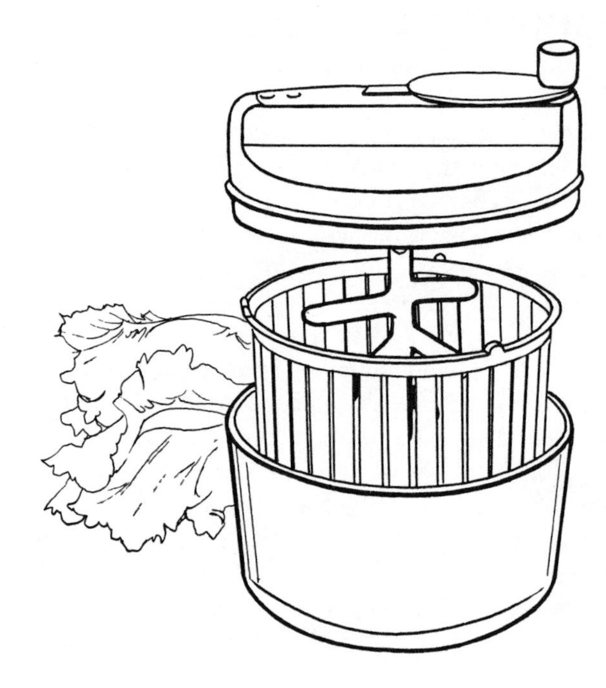

use; while pan is wet, place on the stove and heat. Let cool, and wipe with a little olive oil and a paper towel. Porcelain or enamel pans should be rinsed with hot water after use, and scrubbed with a soft pad. On stainless steel pans, use a scouring powder, and on copper use a commercial copper cleaner.

My **blender, juicer,** and **salad centrifuge** are invaluable aids in my kitchen: the blender to prepare sauces, purées, and other food medleys; the juicer to prepare fruit and vegetable juices, fruit sherbets, and nut butters; and the salad centrifuge to dry washed greens.

The **wok,** once thought an unusual kitchen utensil, has now won acceptance in many kitchens as an irreplaceable tool. I use mine constantly and recommend using it when stir-frying vegetables.

My **cooking forks and spoons** are made of wood—the sound of a metal spoon against a pan while cooking is a sour note in a symphony.

A **nutgrinder** is essential to grind and blend your nuts and seeds to the necessary consistency for optimal digestion. I use a Molinex coffee grinder for this; it works perfectly well.

A **Cuisinart** or other food processing machine can be an excellent addition to your kitchen tools, especially if you routinely cook for large numbers of people. Be sure to adjust your blade according to the preparation instructions given (chopping, mincing, shredding, etc.). Although I don't use one of these machines, I think that is more my artistic preference and a need to stay physically in touch with my food; realistically, a Cuisinart can mean fast and easy food preparation with maximum utilization of resources.

Cuisinart™
FOOD PROCESSOR
CAUTION

Cooking Methods

The secret, when applying heat to vegetables, is to do it efficiently so they will remain firm and crisp and lose as little nutritional value as possbile. I prefer sautíng, baking, and steaming, but simmering and boiling are also useful cooking methods.

Sautéing is very quick stir-frying. The ingredients should be minced or cut thin and placed in a pan sufficiently large so as not to crowd them. Be sure the pan is already hot and that cooking starts as soon as the ingredients are added and continues until the food is tender. The food is stirred constantly to prevent overcooking. This quick, hot cooking sears the food, preventing the juices from escaping.

Baking is the application of dry heat in an oven; the other cooking methods we'll talk about use moist heat. However, for me, baking is never a totally dry process: wrapping foods in foil and using a covered roasting pan allows the moist vapors of the food to surround and permeate the cooking food (except, of course for the delicious aromas that escape to tantalize the hungry cook!) NOTE: All oven temperatures are given in Fahrenheit.

Steaming is cooking food by steam; it's one of my favorite preparation methods. Fancy, store-bought steamers are available, but a metal colander placed in a large pot with a tight-fitting lid is adequate. The water should be boiling before the steamer is set in place. When the vegetables have been added, cover the pan immediately and keep covered until steaming is complete. Bamboo steamers are best used with a wok. Place water in your wok, let boil, put the bamboo steamer inside the wok, add the vegetables to the steamer, and cover. I particularly like this process, as the sweet smell the wet bamboo gives off heightens my delight in preparing and eating the steamed food.

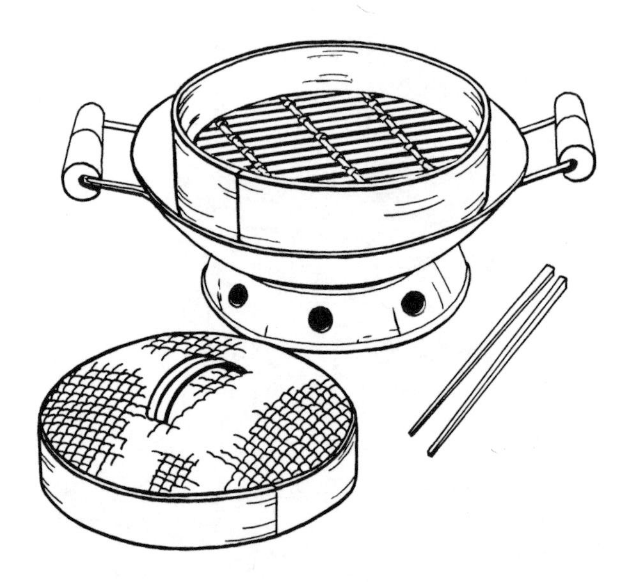

The liquid from steaming, whether in bamboo or metal steamers, should not be thrown down the drain: let it cool and drink it with your meal, or use it in preparing sauces or broths. Many of the essential minerals and other nutrients from the steamed foods are steamed out of the food and into the water. Liquid nutrition!

Simmering is a very gentle and low heating—almost a boil, but not quite. It requires careful attention to be sure that the heat is kept just below boiling. When simmering, delicate foods are cushioned as the tiny bubbles form a gentle, protective covering.

Boiling, on the other hand, is more boisterous; it's a slam-bam way of cooking, best reserved for teas and soups, as the process leaches out many nutritional goodies into the liquid. If you're able to drink the liquid, fine. But boiling involves large quantities of water. In fact, to be sure the process takes as little time as possible, always use sufficient water—at least three times the amount needed to cover what is being boiled.

I use foil for baking potatoes, turnips, and other vegetables, and am unable to detect any metallic taste in the foods so cooked. But it's a method to be used judiciously, I feel, at least until we know more about the effects it might have.

With many of these recipes, the baking process can actually be done in a large skillet on top of your stove, covered tightly and over a low to medium heat. I prefer an oven, but I know its sometimes easier to use the stove top. Be sure to use stainless steel or copper/stainless steel pans.

Eating and Serving Utensils

I prefer chopsticks to a fork; I prefer wooden spoons, or Chinese porcelain spoons, to metal. My drinking utensils bring art to my table: my mugs are lovingly designed and made by potters.

My dishes, plates, bowls, and platters are characterized by their pleasing color, appropriate size, and organically suitable material. I do not eat from paper plates; I do not eat from plastic. In fact, I generally shun plastic in all forms in my kitchen, except for plastic bags which are useful for refrigerating uncooked foods. (And remember when refrigerating cooked foods to always place them in a dish covered with a towel.)

Chapter Five

Garden Green Salads

For garden green salads, select produce that looks freshest and most appealing: unblemished, with bright colors. Produce tastes best and is most nutritious if used as soon as possible after purchase or picking. As a preliminary to salad-making, thoroughly wash and dry all greens. I use a salad centrifuge of the crank or pull type, a vegetable dryer which can be found in most kitchenware shops. Or, more primitively, simply pat greens dry between paper towels or two clean dish towels.
Unless otherwise noted, salad greens should be chopped into small bits. This makes it easier for them to become coated with dressing when tossed, and also makes mastication easier. Remember when eating *any* food to masticate until saliva dominates in the mouth, then swallow. Follow this process before putting another chopstick, fork, or spoon full of food into your mouth.

When choosing ingredients for salad dressings, I kept the following in mind. Honey is a high concentration of sugar and contains formic acid. I use it sparingly in salad dressings or in any food. I prefer cold pressed unrefined virgin olive oil. Other good salad oils are safflower oil or sunflower oil. Raw garlic is high in mustard oil and can be irritating to the digestive system. Use it cautiously. Finally, I encourage the use of nut proteins, soy beans, and all kinds of sprouts in salad dressings.

To prepare and serve the salads that follow, you will need the usual array of salad tools: chopping board and knife, measuring cups and spoons, a salad bowl or other large serving container, and salad utensils. Some of the dressings are best prepared in a blender and are so marked. If you don't have a blender, finely mince and/or mash together the ingredients listed. The consistency may be less smooth, but you will have essentially the same dressing.

All the salad recipes make four to six average-sized portions. You can vary amounts to suit your menu, appetite, and guests. Similarly, the concept "bunch" will differ from store to store, and from eater to eater. Vary amounts to please your palate. As you learn to enjoy the subtle and delicate flavors of Nature's Garden, your palate will become more sensitive and your sense of experimentation more developed.

1) ROMAINE AND RED LETTUCE SALAD

1 head romaine lettuce
1 head red leaf letuce
½ bunch watercress
½ head escarole

Wash ingredients well, dry thoroughly, and chop into small bits. Prepare dressing by mixing together:

½ cup olive oil
juice of 1 lemon
1 tablespoon mineral powder
1 tablespoon nutritional yeast

Toss greenery quickly in a large bowl; add dressing and toss lightly again. Serves four to six.

2) DANDELION SALAD

2 heads bibb lettuce
½ bunch dandelion greens
½ bunch celery
½ large red onion
kernels from 3 ears uncooked corn

Wash all ingredients, dry them well, and chop into small bits. Put together the following in your blender, and mix well:

½ medium avocado
½ medium red tomato, halved
1 teaspoon kelp
1 tablespoon mineral powder
½ bunch sweet basil
½ cup olive oil

Pour dressing over greenery (though not really green in this case. Look at the beautiful mix of colors from the lettuce, onion, and corn. Eat with your eyes too!) Toss well and serve to four hungry friends.

3) SWISS CHARD SALAD

1 bunch Swiss chard
2 large (or 3 small) red bell peppers
1 avocado
½ medium onion
3 cucumbers
1 head butter lettuce
kernels from 3 ears of uncooked corn

Wash all ingredients, dry thoroughly, and chop well. Mix together in a small bowl or jar:

juice of 1 lemon
1 teaspoon rosemary
1 tablespoon mineral powder
½ cup olive oil

Pour dressing over greens and toss quickly in a large bowl; this, as with all my salad recipes, serves four to six.

Since preparations are essentially the same for all the following salads, I will just give very basic instructions, ingredients, and quantities for each form this point. Remember to dry ingredients well, chop well, mix well, and eat well.

4) OAKLEAF SALAD

Clean, chop, and toss:

1 head romaine lettuce
2 large (or 3 small) tomatoes
3 cucumbers
½ bunch kale
½ kohlrabi
1 head oakleaf lettuce

Mix a dressing of:

1 tablespoon mineral powder
1 teaspoon balanced protein seasoning
½ cup olive oil

5) GREEN BEAN SALAD

Clean, chop, and toss:
1 head butter lettuce
½ head romaine lettuce
4 green onions
½ lb. green beans (fresh, not canned—it makes a vast difference)

Mix a dressing of:

1 teaspoon rosemary
1 teaspoon oregano
½ cup olive oil

6) CHICORY AND PEA SALAD

Clean, chop, and toss:

1 head romaine lettuce
1 head red leaf lettuce
½ bunch chicory
1 lb. peas
½ head lamb's lettuce (or lettuce of choice)
kernels from 3 ears uncooked corn

Mix a dressing of:

1 tablespoon almond butter
1 teaspoon mineral powder
½ cup olive oil

7) ROMAINE AND KALE SALAD

Clean, chop, and toss:

1½ heads romaine lettuce
½ bunch kale
½ bunch parsley
½ bunch spinach
½ bunch watercress

Mix in your blender a dressing of:

9 mushrooms
1 teaspoon mineral bouillon
2 cloves garlic
½ cup olive oil

8) RED LEAF AND SPINACH SALAD

Clean, chop, and toss:

½ bunch spinach
2 heads red leaf lettuce
3 cucumbers
½ medium onion
2 Belgian endives

Mix in your blender a dressing of:

9 mushrooms
1 tablespoon cashew butter
3 stalks celery (chop coarsely before putting in blender)
½ cup olive oil

9) ROMAINE AND ANISE SALAD

Clean, chop, and toss:

2 heads romaine lettuce
½ bulb anise
6 stalks asparagus
4 green onions
1 bunch Swiss chard

Mix in your blender a dressing of:

1 lb. peas
½ bunch sweet basil
juice of 1 lemon
½ cup olive oil

10) ROMAINE AND ENDIVE SALAD

Clean, chop, and toss:

1½ heads romaine lettuce
2 Belgian endives
2 red bell peppers
½ bunch spinach
1 bunch garden cress

Mix a dressing of:

1 teaspoon thyme
1 tablespoon mineral powder
½ cup olive oil

11) BEANS AND GREENS

Clean, chop, and toss:

1 head red leaf lettuce
1 head romaine lettuce
½ bunch mustard greens
½ lb. green beans
½ lb. peas
½ red onion

Mix a dressing of:

1 tablespoon mineral powder
1 teaspoon nutritional yeast
1 teaspoon kelp
½ cup olive oil

12) CHICORY AND TURNIP SALAD

Clean, chop, and toss:

1 bunch chicory
1½ heads bibb lettuce
1 turnip, grated
1 beet, peeled and grated
½ avocado
½ lb. peas

Mix a dressing of:

juice of 2 lemons
1 teaspoon lemon thyme
½ cup olive oil

13) ROMAINE AND SPINACH SALAD

Clean, chop, and toss:

2 heads romaine lettuce
½ bunch spinach
1 bunch sweet basil
¼ bunch parsley
4 stalks celery
½ red onion

Mix a dressing of:

½ teaspoon balanced protein seasoning
1 tablespoon mineral powder
½ cup olive oil

14) ROMAINE AND CHAYOTE SALAD

Clean, chop, and toss:

2 heads romaine lettuce
½ chayote
3 green peppers
1 bunch chicory
1 lb. peas

Mix a dressing of:

½ cup raisins
juice of 1 lemon
1 tablespoon mineral powder
½ cup olive oil

15) DIFFERENT POTATO SALAD

Clean, chop, and toss:

1 large potato, grated
1 red onion
5 stalks celery
2 heads red leaf lettuce
1 head bib lettuce

Mix a dressing of:

1 tablespoon mineral powder
1 teaspoon kelp
½ cup olive oil

16) ROMAINE AND RED PEPPERS

Clean, chop, and toss:

2 heads romaine lettuce
½ bunch spinach
½ bunch kale
3 red bell peppers
3 green onions
1 bunch sweet basil
1 turnip, grated

Mix in your blender a dressing of:

½ cup raisins
4 mushrooms
½ bunch parsley
1 tablespoon mineral powder
½ cup olive oil

17) CUCUMBERS AND KALE SALAD

Clean, chop, and toss:

4 cucumbers
½ bunch dandelion greens
½ bunch kale
½ bunch parsley
1 yellow onion

Mix a dressing of:

1 tablespoon almond butter
½ cup olive oil

18) PEPPERS AND SQUASH SALAD

Clean, chop, and toss:

3 sweet red peppers
¼ bunch mustard greens
2 heads romaine lettuce
2 large yellow squash
kernels from 3 ears uncooked corn

Mix a dressing of:

1 tablespoon mineral powder
1 teaspoon kelp
½ teaspoon balanced protein seasoning
½ cup olive oil

19) SQUASH AND LETTUCE SALAD

Clean, chop, and toss:

2 large yellow squash
1 large zucchini
3 green onions
½ bunch spinach
½ bunch Swiss chard
1 head bibb lettuce

Mix in your blender a dressing of:

½ large red bell pepper, coarsely chopped
1 teaspoon almond/cashew butter
½ cup olive oil

20) ROMAINE AND TOMATO SALAD

Clean, chop, and toss:

1 head romaine lettuce
4 cucumbers
½ yellow onion
½ bunch sweet basil
2 tomatoes
1 head oakleaf lettuce (or lettuce of choice)

Mix a dressing of:

½ teaspoon balanced protein seasoning
½ tablespoon mineral powder
½ cup olive oil

21) ALMONDS AND PEAS SALAD

Clean, chop, and toss:

9 mushrooms
2 heads red leaf lettuce
15 chopped almonds
1 lb. sweet peas
½ bunch chicory
kernels from 4 ears uncooked corn

Mix a dressing of:

juice of 1 lemon
1 tablespoon mineral powder
1 teaspoon balanced protein seasoning
½ cup olive oil

22) ROMAINE AND BEET SALAD

Clean, chop, and toss:

2 beets, peeled and sliced
1 red onion
2 heads romaine lettuce
4 cucumbers
¼ bunch Swiss chard
5 stalks celery

Mix a dressing of:

½ bunch parsley
1 clove garlic, minced
juice of 1 lemon
1 tablespoon nutritional yeast
1 teaspoon kelp
½ cup olive oil

23) ROMAINE AND DANDELION GREENS

Clean, chop, and toss:

2 heads romaine lettuce
½ bunch dandelion greens
2 tomatoes
1 red onion
½ bulb anise
kernels from 4 ears uncooked corn

Mix a dressing of:

½ bunch sweet basil
4 mushrooms, minced
½ teaspoon miso
juice of 1 lemon
½ cup olive oil

24) LETTUCE AND CRESS SALAD

Clean, chop, and toss:

1 bunch watercress
4 cucumbers
½ red onion
2 heads romaine lettuce
1 bunch garden cress
kernels from 4 ears uncooked corn

Mix a dressing of:
½ bunch sweet basil
1 teaspoon rosemary
1 teaspoon balanced protein seasoning
½ cup olive oil

25) ROMAINE AND ASPARAGUS SALAD

Clean, chop, and toss:

2 heads romaine lettuce
8 stalks asparagus
4 stalks celery
½ bunch parsley
¼ head mustard greens
2 yellow squash

Mix a dressing of:

1 tablespoon rosemary
1 teaspoon thyme
juice of 1 lemon
1 clove garlic, minced
1 tablespoon mineral powder
½ cup olive oil

26) CRESS AND SQUASH SALAD

Clean, chop, and toss:

3 zucchini
¼ bunch mustard greens
1 lb. peas
½ bunch watercress
½ bunch garden cress
kernels from 4 ears uncooked corn

Mix a dressing of:

1 teaspoon lemon thyme
1 teaspoon sage
juice of 1 lemon
½ teaspoon almond butter
½ cup olive oil

27) PEPPERS AND GREENS

Clean, chop, and toss:

4 red bell peppers
¼ bunch mustard greens
¼ bulb anise
2 heads red leaf lettuce
¼ bunch collard greens
1 beet, peeled

Mix a dressing of:

½ teaspoon fennel seeds
1 tablespoon mineral powder
1 tablespoon nutritional yeast
½ cup olive oil

28) GREEN AND YELLOW SALAD

Clean, chop, and toss:

1 head red leaf lettuce
1 head bibb lettuce
½ head romaine lettuce
½ bunch garden cress
1 Belgian endive
kernels from 6 ears uncooked corn

Mix a dressing of:

1 teaspoon fennel seeds
1 tablespoon almond butter
juice of ½ lime
½ cup olive oil

29) ENDIVE AND OLIVE SALAD

Clean, chop, and toss:

2 Belgian endives
½ bunch sweet basil
10 black olives, pitted
5 mushrooms
2 heads bibb lettuce
1 head oakleaf lettuce
¼ bunch parsley

Mix a dressing of:

1 tablespoon nutritional yeast
juice of ½ lime
juice of ½ lemon
½ teaspoon balanced protein seasoning
½ cup olive oil

30) ROMAINE AND CORN SALAD

Clean, chop, and toss:

2 heads romaine lettuce
2 red bell peppers
4 cucumbers
4 stalks celery
1 bunch garden cress
kernels from 4 ears uncooked corn

Mix in your blender a dressing of:

¼ bunch spinach, chopped
1 tablespoon mineral powder
1 teaspoon kelp
½ cup olive oil

31) TECHNICOLOR SALAD

Clean, chop, and toss:

1 head escarole
2 carrots, grated
1 beet, peeled and grated
1 lb. peas
½ bunch watercress
2 heads bibb lettuce

Mix a dressing of:

1 tablespoon mineral powder
juice of 1 lemon
1 teaspoon kelp
½ cup olive oil

32) ROMAINE AND RADISH SALAD

Clean, chop, and toss:

2 heads romaine lettuce
½ bunch Swiss chard
1 bunch radishes
3 red bell peppers
½ bunch dandelion greens

Mix in your blender a dressing of:

1 green onion, coarsely chopped
1 tablespoon mineral powder
1 teaspoon cashew butter
½ cup olive oil

33) ROMAINE AND CUCUMBER SALAD

Clean, chop, and toss:

3 heads romaine lettuce
6 cucumbers
1 turnip, peeled and grated
½ bunch spinach
¼ bunch parsley

Mix a dressing of:

juice of 1 lemon
1 tablespoon mineral powder
1 teaspoon kelp
½ cup olive oil

34) CABBAGE AND BEET SALAD

Clean, chop, and toss:

¼ head red cabbage
1 beet, peeled and grated
2 heads red leaf lettuce
3 cucumbers
1 bunch garden cress

Mix a dressing of:

1 teaspoon lemon thyme
juice of 1 lemon
½ cup olive oil

35) EGGPLANT AND OLIVE SALAD

Clean, chop, and toss:

½ eggplant, diced small
10 olives, pitted
2 heads romaine lettuce
10 mushrooms
½ avocado

Mix a dressing of:

1 teaspoon rosemary
½ teaspoon sage
½ teaspoon balanced protein seasoning
juice of ½ lemon
½ cup olive oil

36) CABBAGE AND CUCUMBER

Clean, chop, and toss:

¼ head cabbage
6 cucumbers
4 red bell peppers
¼ bunch parsley
2 heads butter lettuce
1 bunch garden cress

Mix a dressing of:

juice of 1 lemon
1 tablespoon mineral powder
1 teaspoon kelp
½ cup olive oil

37) REDS AND GREENS

Clean, chop, and toss:

½ lb. pole beans (diced small)
¼ bunch mustard greens
2 tomatoes
½ bulb anise
2 heads Boston (or butterhead) lettuce

Mix a dressing of:

½ teaspoon thyme
½ bunch sweet basil
½ cup olive oil

38) SPINACH AND TURNIP SALAD:

Clean, chop, and toss:

6 turnips, peeled and grated
3 bunches spinach

Mix a dressing of:

juice of 1 lemon
3 cloves garlic, minced
½ cup olive oil

39) AVOCADO SALAD

Clean, chop, and toss:

2 avocados
2 heads red leaf lettuce
3 Belgian endives
3 green onions

Mix a dressing of:

1 tablespoon mineral powder
½ cup olive oil

40) BIBB AND BEAN SALAD

Clean, chop, and toss:

½ lb. green beans
½ lb. peas
6 cucumbers
½ bulb anise
½ bunch spinach
1 head bibb lettuce

Mix a dressing of:

½ teaspoon sage
juice of 1 lemon
½ cup olive oil

41) AVOCADO AND TOMATO SALAD

Clean, chop, and toss:

3 avocados
4 tomatoes
6 cucumbers
4 green onions
kernels from 3 ears uncooked corn

Mix a dressing of:

1 teaspoon lemon thyme
½ teaspoon rosemary
½ cup olive oil

42) AVOCADO AND CUCUMBER SALAD

Clean, chop, and toss:

3 tomatoes
1 bunch sweet basil
3 green onions
5 cucumbers
3 avocados

Mix a dressing of:

1 teaspoon kelp
1 tablespoon mineral powder
1 teaspoon balanced protein seasoning
½ cup olive oil

43) CUKES AND ZUKES

Clean, chop, and toss:

6 cucumbers
2 zucchini
1 red onion
2 avocados
1 lb. string beans

Mix a dressing of:

1 tablespoon mineral powder
juice of 1 lemon
½ cup olive oil

44) LIMA BEANS AND BRUSSELS SPROUTS SALAD

Clean, chop, and toss:

2 bunches garden cress
3 tomatoes
2 red onions
10 Brussels sprouts
1 lb. lima beans

Mix a dressing of:

juice of ½ lemon
1 teaspoon rosemary
½ cup olive oil

45) TOMATOES AND ANISE SALAD

Clean, chop, and toss:

6 tomatoes
2 red onions
6 cucumbers
1 bulb anise

Mix a dressing of:

1 teaspoon oregano
½ cup olive oil

46) BIBB AND ENDIVE SALAD

Clean, chop, and toss:

2 Belgian endives
5 olives (black or green), left whole
1 head romaine lettuce
10 mushrooms
2 avocados
1½ heads bibb lettuce

Mix a dressing of:

1 teaspoon thyme
juice of 1 lemon
1 tablespoon mineral powder
½ cup olive oil

47) TOMATOES AND PEAS SALAD

Clean, chop, and toss:

2 tomatoes
1 Belgian endive
3 green onions
1 lb. peas
½ bunch chicory
1 head escarole

Mix a dressing of:

1 teaspoon lemon thyme
½ teaspoon oregano
1 tablespoon nutritional yeast
½ cup olive oil

48) LIMA BEANS AND LETTUCE SALAD

Clean, chop, and toss:

½ lb. baby lima beans (fresh, not dried)
2 heads romaine lettuce
¼ bunch parsley
½ head fennel
½ head red leaf lettuce
kernels from 6 ears uncooked corn

Mix a dressing of:

½ teaspoon sage
1 bunch sweet basil
½ cup olive oil

49) CHICORY AND CUCUMBERS

Clean, chop, and toss:

1 head bibb lettuce
2 tomatoes
6 mushrooms
6 cucumbers
1 red onion
1 bunch chicory

Mix a dressing of:

1 tablespoon mineral powder
1 teaspoon balanced protein seasoning
½ cup olive oil

Raw and Cooked Salads

These salads combine raw and cooked vegetables. For easiest preparation, fix the cooked vegetables first; then place them in your salad bowl to cool. Meanwhile, prepare the raw vegetables. Add dressing to the cooked vegetables, then add the raw vegetables, and mix well together. It's best to refrigerate these salads before serving.

Besides the utensils mentioned earlier for salad preparation, you'll need a covered roasting pan, a covered pan (either with steamer or collander), and a skillet. All raw vegetables should be chopped small; cooked vegetables may be chopped to the extent that pleases you.

50) BROCCOLI AND LETTUCE SALAD

Steam in 4 oz. water and 1 tablespoon mineral bouillon, 10 minutes:

1 bunch broccoli
½ lb. Brussels sprouts

Clean, chop, and toss raw ingredients:

2 heads butter lettuce
3 green onions
kernels from 4 ears uncooked corn

Mix raw and cooked ingredients together.

Mix a dressing of:

1 tablespoon mineral powder
1 teaspoon balanced protein seasoning
½ cup olive oil

51) SWEET POTATOES AND GREENS

Preheat oven to 450° for 10 minutes. Bake separately in tinfoil or together in a covered baking dish for 30 minutes:

1 large sweet potato
1 red onion

Clean, chop, and toss raw ingredients:

1 head romaine lettuce
½ bunch garden cress
½ bunch spinach
1 head bibb lettuce

Mix raw and cooked ingredients together.

Mix a dressing of:

1 teaspoon rosemary
1 tablespoon mineral powder
½ cup olive oil

52) BRUSSELS SPROUTS AND LETTUCE SALAD

Steam in 4 oz. water and 2 tablespoons mineral powder:

½ lb. Brussels sprouts
1 lb. peas

Clean, chop, and toss raw ingredients:

3 green onions
2 heads red leaf lettuce
1 avocado
kernels from 4 ears uncooked corn

Mix raw and cooked ingredients together.

Mix a dressing of:

juice of 1 lemon
1 teaspoon rosemary
½ cup olive oil

53) GREEN BEANS AND ZUCCHINI SALAD

Steam in 2 oz. mineral bouillon, 4 oz. water, 2 oz. olive oil:

2 sliced chayote (5 minutes)
1½ lb. green beans (7 minutes)

Clean, chop, and toss raw ingredients:

¼ head cabbage
2 heads red leaf lettuce
2 large zucchini
3 cucumbers

Mix raw and cooked ingredients together.

Mix a dressing of:

1 tablespoon mineral powder
1 tablespoon nutritional yeast
½ cup olive oil

54) EGGPLANT AND GREENS

Preheat oven at 450° for 10 minutes. Reduce to 350° and bake for 15 minutes in a covered roasting pan:

1 eggplant, diced small
4 small zucchini, diced

Clean, chop, and toss raw ingredients:

2 heads romaine lettuce
½ bunch dandelion greens
½ bunch chicory
3 green onions

Mix raw and cooked ingredients together.

Mix a dressing of:

1 tablespoon mineral powder
½ cup olive oil

55) CAULIFLOWER AND BROCCOLI

Steam in 4 oz. water, 4 oz. olive oil, and 2 tablespoons mineral powder for 5 minutes:

1 head cauliflower, chopped
1 bunch broccoli, chopped

Clean, chop, and toss raw ingredients:

2 tomatoes
1 head bibb lettuce
½ red onion
1 avocado

Mix a dressing of:

1 tablespoon mineral powder
1 tablespoon nutritional yeast
½ cup olive oil

56) EGGPLANT AND BELL PEPPER SALAD

Preheat oven at 450° for 10 minutes. Reduce to 350° and bake for 15 minutes in a covered roasting pan:

2 eggplants, sliced
1 teaspoon mineral bouillon
4 oz. water
4 oz. olive oil

Clean, chop, and toss raw ingredients:

1 head butter lettuce
½ head red leaf lettuce
1 red onion
3 green bell peppers
kernels from 3 ears uncooked corn

Mix raw and cooked ingredients together.

Mix a dressing of:

1 tablespoon mineral powder
1 teaspoon balanced protein seasoning
½ cup olive oil

57) LIMAS AND LETTUCE

Steam in ½ teaspoon mineral bouillon and 4 oz. water:

1 lb. lima beans, 10 minutes
1 lb. asparagus, 'til barely tender

Clean, chop, and toss raw ingredients:

1 head oakleaf lettuce
3 red bell peppers
3 green onions
1 head bibb lettuce
1 bunch dandelion greens

Mix raw and cooked ingredients together.

Mix a dressing of:

1 tablespoon mineral powder
1 tablespoon nutritional yeast
1 teaspoon SeaZun
½ cup olive oil

58) RUTABAGAS AND RED LEAF SALAD

Steam in ½ teaspoon mineral bouillon, 4 oz. water, 2 tablespoons mineral powder, and 2 oz. olive oil:

2 large rutabagas
12 water chestnuts

Clean, chop, and toss raw ingredients:

1 turnip, peeled and grated
½ bunch spinach
2 heads red leaf lettuce
3 cucumbers

Mix raw and cooked ingredients together.

Mix a dressing of:

1 teaspoon lemon thyme
½ teaspoon sage
½ cup olive oil

59) SWEET POTATO, SPINACH, AND ONION SALAD

Steam in 4 oz. water for 3 minutes:

2 bunches spinach

Bake for ½ hour:

1 large (or 2 small) sweet potato

Clean, chop, and toss raw ingredients:

1 head romaine lettuce
3 green onions
1 red onion
1 clove garlic
kernels from 3 ears uncooked corn

Mix raw and cooked ingredients together.

Mix a dressing of:

1 tablespoon mineral powder
½ cup olive oil

60) RED, YELLOW, AND GREEN SALAD

Sauté in 2 oz. olive oil, pinch of mineral powder, and 2 oz. water for 6 minutes:

2 beets, diced
6 large carrots, diced

Clean, chop and toss raw vegetables:

½ bunch spinach
3 cucumbers
1 head red leaf lettuce
1 head butter lettuce
kernels from 3 ears uncooked corn

Mix raw and cooked ingredients together.

Mix a dressing of:

1 bunch sweet basil
juice of 1 lemon
1 teaspoon SeaZun
½ cup olive oil

61) ASPARAGUS AND RED LEAF LETTUCE

Sauté in ½ teaspoon mineral bouillon, 4 oz. water, and 2 oz. olive oil for 5 minutes:

1 lb. asparagus, chopped
2 large potatoes, cubed

Clean, chop, and toss raw ingredients:

1 head red leaf lettuce
½ bunch parsley
1 Belgian endive
½ bunch chicory
½ bunch garden cress

Mix raw and cooked ingredients together.

Mix a dressing of:

1 tablespoon mineral powder
1 tablespoon nutritional yeast
1 teaspoon balanced protein seasoning
½ cup olive oil

62) KALE AND HEARTY SALAD

Sauté in ½ teaspoon mineral bouillon, 4 oz. olive oil, 4 oz. water:

1 lb. string beans (10 minutes)
2 bunches spinach (3 minutes)

Clean, chop and toss raw ingredients:

½ bunch chicory
½ bunch kale
2 tomatoes
½ red onion
1 head butter lettuce

Mix a dressing of:

rosemary, to taste
thyme, to taste
½ teaspoon kelp
½ cup olive oil

Chapter Six

Complementing Courses

In keeping with the Salade concept, our universal menu does not include a main course of meat, fish, or fowl. Replacing this is our complementing course which, as its name implies, complements those foods eaten before and after. It alone is not meant to be the focal point of the meal; the combinations of the various flavors and textures of all the foods eaten should provide a complete gastronomic experience.

These recipes are examples of what I have experienced and want to share with you. The results of your inquiry and experimentation will be your finest trip, one that you will want to share with others as you become more aware of the nutritional wonderland of Nature's Garden.

ARTICHOKE ASPARANUT

Gather together these ingredients:

8 artichokes
5 cloves garlic, whole
2 stalks celery, finely chopped
3 slices fresh ginger root
1 tablespoon mineral powder
2 tablespoons miso
½ lemon
2 bunches asparagus, (ends finely chopped, tips and 2 inches of stem left whole)
2 leeks, chopped
¼ lb. mushrooms, chopped
2 cucumbers, finely chopped
½ lb. peas
⅛ lb. each, almonds and cashews (blended together in blender)
¼ cube soya butter
olive oil
water

Cut tips and stems from artichokes and remove the outer two rows of leaves. Spread the artichokes open like flowers and place in a large pot with garlic, celery, ginger root, mineral powder, miso, lemon juice (squeeze juice onto artichokes and drop the lemon rind into the cooking water), and 16 oz. water. Cover and cook over a high flame until water boils. Then lower flame, keep covered, and continue to cook for 10 to 20 minutes. When done, drain artichoke liquid into a bowl; add soya butter to artichokes. Leave artichokes in covered pan while you sauté asparagus, leeks, mushrooms, and cucumbers over a low flame in 2 oz. olive oil and 1 oz. water for 3 minutes. When vegetables are cooked add peas and nut mixture. Remove the larger asparagus pieces and place on a flat serving platter. Stuff the artichokes with half the vegetables and blended nuts. Top each artichoke with a tablespoon of artichoke liquid. Put the rest of the vegetables and blended nuts over the asparagus. Arrange artichokes around the edge of the platter and serve.

IMPROVISATIONS: You can use the remaining broth as a dip for the artichoke leaves, or pour it over the vegetable and nut mixture.

ARTICHOKE GARDENIA

Gather together these ingredients:

8 artichokes
4 large tomatoes, chopped
6 cloves garlic, minced
½ bunch parsley, minced
½ bunch sweet basil, chopped
1 teaspoon sage
1 teaspoon oregano
½ cube soya butter
1 loaf whole wheat sourdough bread
½ lb. mushrooms, chopped
5 black olives, pitted and chopped
2 tablespoons mineral powder
olive oil
water

Preheat oven at 450° for 10 minutes. Cut bread in small pieces and spread on bottom of a roasting pan. Reduce oven to 300° and bake bread cubes for 7 to 8 minutes. Remove from oven, put cubes into blender, and make bread crumbs (if you do not have a blender, place baked bread cubes between sheets of waxed paper and roll with a rolling pin). Set crumbs aside while you prepare artichokes. Cut tips and stems from artichokes; and steam artichokes in a covered pan for 10 to 20 minutes with mineral powder, 2 oz. olive oil, and 16 oz. water. While artichokes are cooking, sauté tomatoes, garlic, parsley, sweet basil, sage, and oregano in 2 oz. olive oil in a covered skillet for 5 to 7 minutes. Then add soya butter and let melt. In another pan, sauté mushrooms and olives for 5 minutes in 1 oz. water and ½ oz. olive oil. Mix tomato sauce with bread crumbs; then add mushrooms and olives. Remove artichokes from pan, drain well, and stuff with tomato-crumb-mushroom mixture. Serve.

ASPARAGUS IN CREPES

Gather together these ingredients:

8 thin homemade crepes (see section on grains)
1½ lbs. asparagus
2 red onions, chopped fine
2 red peppers, chopped fine
¼ lb. mushrooms, sliced fine
2 tomatoes (hand-squeezed)
¼ lb. olives (either black or green), pitted and halved
2 yellow squash, diced
2 zucchini, diced
olive oil
water

Preheat oven at 450° for 10 minutes. Put all ingredients, except crepes, in a covered roasting pan, with 3 oz. olive oil and 2 oz. water. Reduce heat to 300° and cook vegetables for 8 to 10 minutes. Remove pan from the oven; carefully lift out asparagus spears and place a few inside each crepe. Roll each crepe around asparagus spears and place on a serving platter. Cover with the remaining vegetables and their stock. Serve.

ASPARAGUS HIDDEN IN A HUBBARD SQUASH

Gather together these ingredients:

1 large Hubbard squash
1½ lbs. asparagus, chopped
3 cucumbers, thinly sliced
1 lb. peas
2 bunches spinach
4 oz. mineral bouillon
olive oil
water

Preheat oven at 450° for 10 minutes. Carefully cut off the top of the squash and scrape out the insides into a bowl. Set aside. Put the top of the squash, or "cap," and the hollowed-out squash in a covered roasting pan. Add a stock of 2 oz. mineral bouillon and 6 oz. water. Reduce oven heat to 300° and bake squash for 30 to 40 minutes. Meanwhile, sauté the asparagus stalks in an open skillet with 2 oz. mineral bouillon, 2 oz. olive oil, and 2 oz. water for 3 to 5 minutes. Then add the cucumbers and peas, and sauté for 2 to 3 minutes. Add 1 cube safflower butter, let melt, and mix well. Steam spinach in an open skillet for 2 to 3 minutes with 2 oz. water. Finely chop cooked spinach and add to cooked asparagus. Remove the squash from the oven; stuff firmly the hollowed-out squash with the asparagus-spinach mixture. Put on the cap, cut the squash in thick round slices, and serve.

IMPROVISATIONS: You can lightly sauté the squash insides, minus seeds, in ¼ cube safflower butter and 1 tablespoon miso and serve with your squash rounds as a separate dish.

BROCCOLI AND EGGPLANT IN A GREEN VEIL

Gather together these ingredients:

5 heads broccoli
3 medium eggplants, cubed
4 green onions, chopped
2 bunches fresh mustard greens
2 cloves garlic, minced
1 Belgian endive, thinly sliced
1 cube safflower butter
1 tablespoon mineral powder
1 oz. mineral bouillon
2 teaspoons kelp
olive oil
water

Chop broccoli tops into quarters and stems into small pieces. In your wok, make a stock of kelp, 1 oz. olive oil, and 1 oz. water. Add broccoli and sauté over a high flame, quickly and constantly stirring for 5 minutes. Put cubed eggplants, green onions, and garlic in a separate pan with 2 oz. olive oil and 1 oz. water. Sauté until eggplant is cooked, about 5 to 7 minutes. Steam mustard greens (slice off and discard woody part of stems) in 2 oz. water, mineral powder, and mineral bouillon for 3 minutes. When cooked, add cube of safflower butter; let melt, and toss lightly. Mix broccoli with eggplant cubes and place on a long serving platter. Dribble stock over all. Cover with mustard greens and stock. Top with Belgian endive, and serve.

BROCCOLI AND RED PEPPERS IN RAW AND COOKED MUSHROOM SAUCE

Gather together these ingredients:

4 heads broccoli
6 red bell peppers, chopped
4 green onions, chopped
4 turnips
½ lb. fresh mushrooms
½ bunch parsley
¼ bunch garden cress
10 black olives
1 stalk celery, chopped
1 teaspoon mineral powder
1 oz. mineral bouillon
olive oil
water

Preheat oven at 450° for 10 minutes. Wrap each turnip separately in tinfoil; reduce oven to 350° and bake turnips for 15 to 20 minutes. Slice the broccoli in long thin strips from flower to stem and place with peppers and onions in a roasting pan. Bake for 8 to 10 minutes.

While turnips and broccoli mix are baking, sauté for 5 to 8 minutes ¼ lb. mushrooms (that's half of the mushrooms you've gathered) in mineral powder, 1 oz. olive oil, and ½ oz. water. After sautéing, drain stock into your blender and add the other ¼

lb. of raw mushrooms, and the parsley, garden cress, celery, olives, and mineral bouillon. Blend well and add to the cooked mushrooms. Remove the broccoli mix and the turnips from the oven. Place the broccoli mix on a serving platter, set the whole turnips around them (removed from foil, naturally), and top the broccoli and peppers with the mushroom sauce. Serve.

This blend of flavors is perfectly set off by the delights of a sauce presenting the intriguing flavors of both raw and sautéed mushrooms.

BROCCOLI IN WHEAT DISCS

Gather together these ingredients:

4 to 6 whole wheat discs (see section on grains)
4 bunches broccoli
3 red onions, thinly sliced
2 heads cauliflower, chopped
2 large tomatoes, chopped
3 stalks celery, chopped
2 cloves garlic, chopped
1 tablespoon mineral powder
1 tablespoon miso
½ cube soya butter
kernels of 2 ears uncooked corn
olive oil
water

Preheat oven at 450° for 10 minutes. Chop the broccoli—the stems finely, the flowers in small chunks. Put broccoli in covered roasting pan with onions and cauliflower. Blend mineral powder and miso together with 6 oz. water and pour over vegetables. Reduce oven to 300° and bake for 8 to 12 minutes. Meanwhile, sauté tomatoes, celery, and garlic in a covered skillet with 2 oz. olive oil and 1 oz. water. After 5 minutes add soya butter and corn; mix well. Remove baked vegetables form oven; put vegetables and whole wheat discs (chopped into quarters) in a large serving dish. Cover with tomato sauce; mix together well. Serve.

BRUSSELS SPROUTS

Gather together these ingredients:

2 lbs. Brussels sprouts
½ head red cabbage, finely chopped
2 red onions, chopped
5 carrots, diced
2 russet potatoes, diced
1 oz. mineral bouillon
2 tablespoons mineral powder
olive oil
water

Preheat oven at 450° for 10 minutes. Prepare an onion sauce: put chopped onions into a covered roasting pan with 3 oz. water, 2 oz. olive oil, mineral bouillon, and mineral powder. Reduce oven to 350° and bake onions for 3 minutes. While onion sauce is cooking, trim Brussels sprouts, removing stems and any blemished leaves. Add Brussels sprouts and chopped cabbage to the onion sauce and bake for another 5 to 8 minutes.

Meanwhile, sauté diced carrots and potatoes in 2 oz. olive oil and 1 oz. water for 5 to 8 minutes. Remove Brussels sprouts and cabbage from oven and place in a large serving dish. Cover with sautéed vegetables, and serve.

CABBAGE AND BAKED SWEET POTATO CREAM

Gather together these ingredients:

2 heads Chinese cabbage, thickly cubed
2 large sweet potatoes
1 stem bamboo shoot, sliced
4 green onions, chopped
1 lb. lima beans
½ lb. peas
½ bunch mint leaves, chopped
½ bunch parsley, chopped
1 tablespoon mineral powder
1 tablespoon miso
½ bunch sweet basil, chopped
¼ cube soya butter
olive oil
water

Preheat oven at 450° for 10 minutes. Wrap unpeeled sweet potatoes in tinfoil; reduce oven to 400° and bake potatoes for 25 minutes. Combine bamboo shoot, onions, beans, and peas in a stock of mineral powder, miso, basil, 1 oz. olive oil, and 3 oz. water. Sauté in a covered skillet over a low flame for 5 to 7 minutes. When vegetables are cooked, drain the stock into your wok. Add soya butter and 1 oz. olive oil to the vegetables and mix well. Add the cubed cabbage to the wok and cook over a medium flame for about 3 to 5 minutes, stirring frequently. When cabbage is cooked, put the other sautéed vegetables into the wok, turn off the flame, and cover tightly so as not to release any flavors.

Take the sweet potatoes from the oven and carefully remove the skins and mix. Mash the potatoes well and add the skins and parsley. Put the cabbage and cooked vegetables into a large serving bowl and top with the mashed sweet potatoes, giving the appearance of sweet orange topping. Sprinkle with chopped mint leaves, and serve.

CABBAGE SAVOY

Gather together these ingredients:

2 large heads savoy cabbage
6 yellow squash, chopped
5 shallots, chopped
½ eggplant, peeled and chopped
2 bunches chicory
4 cloves garlic
¼ lb. walnuts or pecans, shelled
juice of 2 lemons
1 tablespoon mineral powder
1 large yellow onion
olive oil
water

Remove and discard the coarse outer leaves from the cabbage; steam both heads, whole, in a large covered pan with the whole onion, mineral powder, lemon juice, 1 oz. olive oil, and 3 oz. water. Use a low flame and cook for about 8 to 12 minutes. Meanwhile, sauté squash, shallots, and eggplant in 1 oz. olive oil and 1 oz. water for 8 to 10 minutes. Keep skillet covered, but stir frequently.

In another pan, heat whole garlic and water together for 3 to 5 minutes over a very low flame. Then add chicory and steam for 3 minutes. When cooked, chop both the chicory and garlic. Mix together sautéed vegetables, chopped chicory and garlic, and nuts in a savory dressing. Remove cabbage heads from pan, spread leaves carefully and stuff with stuffing. Fold leaves up and around and tie together with a string. Serve.

IMPROVISATIONS: If you wish, return stuffed cabbage to steaming pan and cook for another 3 to 5 minutes over a low flame.

CABBAGE IN TOMATO SAUCE

Gather together these ingredients:

1 savoy cabbage, thickly cubed
1 Chinese cabbage, thickly cubed
1 bunch Chinese broccoli, coarsely chopped
2 large yellow tomatoes
1 large red tomato
4 cloves garlic, minced
3 stalks celery, chopped
6 shallots, chopped
1 bunch parsley, minced
1 teaspoon rosemary
½ lb. mushrooms, sliced
2 Belgian endives, chopped
2 cucumbers, chopped
1 bunch garden cress, chopped
6 carrots, diced
1 teaspoon lemon thyme
1 oz. mineral bouillon
juice of 1 lemon
olive oil
water

Sauté over a low flame the yellow and red tomatoes (hand-squeezed), garlic, celery, shallots, parsley, rosemary, lemon thyme, and mineral bouillon in 2 oz. olive oil in a covered skillet. After 3 minutes add broccoli and both cabages, cover again, and cook for another 5 to 8 minutes. In a second skillet, sauté mushrooms, endives, cucumbers, garden cress, and carrots in lemon juice, 1 oz. water, and 1 oz. olive oil for 4 to 6 minutes. Place cooked cabbage and broccoli and their tomato sauce in the center of a large serving dish. Surround with sautéed vegetables, and serve.

CARROTS IN A BED OF GREENS

Gather together these ingredients:

10 carrots
4 stalks celery, finely chopped
1 bunch mustard greens, coarsely chopped
2 bunches escarole, coarsely chopped
½ bunch garden cress, chopped
½ bunch parsley, chopped
10 black olives, chopped
2 tomatoes, thinly sliced
1 cucumber, thinly sliced
juice of 3 lemons
1 teaspoon mineral bouillon
2 teaspoons kelp
1 cube soya butter
olive oil
water

Preheat oven at 450° for 10 minutes. Cut carrots in pointed slices (Oriental fashion) and place in a covered roasting pan with celery. Add a stock of 2 oz. olive oil and 4 oz. water; reduce oven to 300° and bake vegetables for 8 to 10 minutes. When vegetables are tender, add soya butter and let melt. In a wok, sauté together kelp, mineral bouillon, lemon juice, 2 oz. olive oil, and 3 oz. water for a few minutes. Add mustard greens and escarole and stir-fry for about 3 minutes. When greens are cooked, add garden cress, parsley, and olives; mix well. Place carrots on a long serving platter and cover with greens. Top with slices of tomatoes and cucumber. Serve.

CARROTS AND VEGETABLES IN A CARROT SAUCE

Gather together these ingrdients:
16 medium carrots
6 zucchini, sliced
3 yellow squash, sliced
6 shallots, sliced
1 bunch escarole, chopped
kernels from 5 ears uncooked corn
1 tablespoon carrot syrup
1 teaspoon mineral powder
1 oz. mineral bouillon
½ bunch mint leaves
1 teaspoon cashew butter
olive oil
water

Preheat oven at 450° for 10 minutes. Place whole carrots in a covered roasting pan with carrot syrup, mineral powder, mint leaves, 2 oz. olive oil, and 4 oz. water. Reduce oven to 300° and bake for 8 to 10 minutes. Sauté zucchini, yellow squash, and shallots in mineral bouillon, 1 oz. olive oil, and 1 oz. water for about 6 to 8 minutes. At the last three minutes of cooking, add escarole. When carrots are cooked, remove from oven, and put 4 of the carrots into a blender. Add corn and cashew butter and blend, adding just enough carrot stock to give blended mixture a paste-like consistency. Spread the carrots on a serving platter and top with the blended sauce. Surround with the cooked vegetables, and serve.

CARROTS AND SWEET POTATO

Gather together these ingredients:

8 carrots
1 large sweet potato
1 lb. asparagus
½ lb. mushrooms, sliced
4 large beets
3 stalks celery, finely chopped
10 large green olives, finely chopped
2 chives, finely chopped
½ lb. tofu, drained
2 oz. mineral bouillon
1 cube soya butter
1 teaspoon mineral powder
1 teaspoon kelp
1 teaspoon carrot syrup
water

Preheat oven at 450° for 10 minutes. Slice carrots lengthwise in three even slices. Cut sweet potato into six slices and put carrots and sweet potato in a covered roasting pan with carrot syrup, mineral bouillon, and 3 oz. water. Reduce oven to 350° and bake for 10 to 12 minutes. Sauté asparagus and mushrooms in soya butter and 2 oz. water over a low flame in a covered skillet for 3 to 5 minutes. Steam beets for 8 to 10 minutes in mineral powder, kelp, and 3 oz. water. Then slice each beet into three large pieces. In a bowl, combine celery, olives, chives, and tofu. Remove carrots and potato from oven and add their stock to tofu mix. Spread sweet potato slices on serving platter and cover with carrots, asparagus, mushrooms, and beets. Top with tofu preparation, and serve.

CAULIFLOWER BOUQUET

Gather together these ingredients:

4 heads cauliflower
1 tomato
3 cloves garlic
¼ lb. Greek olives
1 teaspoon lemon thyme
4 bay leaves
3 slices ginger root
1 tablespoon mineral powder
1 lb. Brussels sprouts
1 lb. baby lima beans (frozen or fresh)
½ lb. peas
1 oz. mineral bouillon
kernels from 4 ears uncooked corn
1 cube soya butter
½ lb. mushrooms, finely chopped
½ bunch sweet basil
5 shallots, chopped
olive oil
water

Preheat oven at 450° for 10 minutes. Cut off and discard the outer leaves and flowers from the cauliflower; place cauliflower heads in a roasting pan. Cover with a stock of whole tomato, garlic, Greek olives, lemon thyme, bay leaves, ginger root, mineral powder, 2 oz. olive oil, and 3 oz. water. Cover, reduce oven to 350° and bake for 8 to 12 minutes. Meanwhile, sauté Brussels sprouts, lima beans, and peas in mineral bouillon, 2 oz. olive oil, and 2 oz. water. After 5 to 7 minutes, add corn kernels and ½ cube soya butter. Remove cauliflower from oven and spoon several ounces of the stock into a skillet with mushrooms, basil, and shallots; sauté them for 3 to 5 minutes. Then add ½ cube soya butter. Place cauliflower on a large serving platter, top with the mushroom sauce, and surround with the sautéed vegetables. Serve.

CAULIFLOWER UNDER GREEN

Gather together these ingredients:

2 heads cauliflower, quartered
1 bunch dandelion greens, finely chopped
1 tablespoon sesame seeds
1 teaspoon balanced protein seasoning
½ lb. okra
1 bunch parsley, finely chopped
5 shallots, chopped
2 cloves garlic, minced
1 cube soya butter
1 bunch Swiss chard
½ lb. peas
olive oil
water

In a small bowl combine balanced protein seasoning, sesame seeds, 2 oz. olive oil, and 3 oz. water. Heat empty wok over a medium flame for 2 minutes. Add stock, and heat for 3 minutes. Add cauliflower; keep cover on as much as possible but do toss cauliflower repeatedly until cooked, no more than 5 minutes. Then add dandelion greens, mix, and cook for 3 more minutes.

Meanwhile, prepare an okra-parsley sauce: trim okra and sauté with parsley in a stock of shallots, garlic, soya butter, 1 oz. olive oil, and 2 oz. water for 3 to 5 minutes. Place in your blender and blend to a cream. Remove and drain cauliflower and dandelion greens from wok and spread on a serving platter. In the stock that remains in your wok, quickly sauté—for 3 minutes—Swiss chard and peas. Surround cauliflower with these vegetables and top with creamy okra-parsley sauce. Serve.

CAULIFLOWER IN SWEET ANISE

Gather together these ingredients:

2 heads cauliflower
1 lb. stringbeans
10 small beets, cubed
2 oz. mineral bouillon
½ cube soya butter
2 cucumbers, peeled and mashed
1 bulb anise, finely chopped
4 stalks celery, chopped
3 large green bell peppers, chopped
1 tablespoon almond butter
2 tablespoons mineral powder
1 bunch mustard greens, chopped
olive oil
water

Preheat oven at 450° for 10 minutes. Cut off and discard the outer leaves and flowers and then quarter each cauliflower. Place a stock of mineral bouillon, soya butter, cucumbers, and 1 oz. olive oil in a large roasting pan and add quartered cauliflower, stringbeans, and beets. Reduce oven to 350° and bake for 10 to 12 minutes. Meanwhile, sauté anise, celery, and peppers in a stock of mineral powder, 1 oz. olive oil, and 2 oz. water for 3 to 5 minutes. Add almond butter and mix well. When cauliflower is tender, remove roasting pan from oven and use some of the stock to steam the mustard greens in a covered pan for 3 minutes. Place cauliflower, beans and beets in a serving dish; top with steamed mustard greens; pour anise sauce over all and serve.

EGGPLANT EASY

Gather together these ingredients:

3 eggplants, peeled and diced
2 red bell peppers, diced
3 green onions, chopped
2 bunches spinach
3 slices ginger root
1 tablespoon miso
1 tablespoon sesame seeds
½ cube soya butter
olive oil
water

Make a stock in your wok of ginger slices, miso, 2 oz. olive oil, and 3 oz. water. Heat briefly over a low flame; add eggplant, peppers, and onions. Sauté vegetables over a medium flame for 5 to 7 minutes, turning often.

Meanwhile, steam spinach in 2 oz. water for 3 minutes. Put cooked spinach (still bright green and crunchy) in a bowl and chop into small bits. Add sesame seeds and soya butter. Stir, allowing butter to melt. Add spinach to eggplant mixture in wok. Mix well together, then spoon into serving dish. Serve.

DICED EGGPLANTS

Gather together these ingredients:

4 eggplants
4 cloves garlic, chopped
1 lb. asparagus, finely chopped
2 tomatoes, finely chopped
¼ lb. mushrooms, finely chopped
4 green onions, finely chopped
¼ lb. green olives, pitted and chopped
1 bunch garden cress, chopped
1 avocado, chopped
2 bunches mustard greens
1 oz. mineral bouillon
1 teaspoon rosemary
1 teaspoon mineral powder
olive oil
water

Preheat oven at 450° for 10 minutes. Halve the eggplants horizontally. Without breaking the outer skin, cut squares into the meat, making the impression of a checkerboard. Stuff the chopped garlic pieces into the diced cuts and put the eggplant halves into a roasting pan. In a small bowl, prepare a stock of mineral bouillon, 2 oz. olive oil, and 1½ oz. water. Pour this over the eggplant halves, reduce the oven to 350°, cover, and bake for 10 to 12 minutes.

Meanwhile sauté asparagus, tomatoes, mushrooms, and green onions in 2 oz. olive oil for 5 to 8 minutes. In a bowl mash together the olives, garden cress, rosemary, and avocado until creamy. Steam the mustard greens in a covered pan for 3 minutes in 3 oz. water. When the greens are just barely tender, drain, and add mineral powder and 1 oz. olive oil. Toss lightly, then coarsely chop mustard greens while they are still in the cooking pan.

Now combine the 4 pans of food: remove eggplant halves from oven and fill with asparagus preparation. Top with the avocado mixture and surround with mustard greens. Serve.

ROLLED EGGPLANT WITH GREEN SAUCE

Gather together these ingredients:

3 eggplants, peeled and sliced
3 tomatoes, thinly sliced
¼ lb. black olives, minced
2 bunches spinach, finely chopped
1 bunch escarole, finely chopped
3 zucchini, diced
1 Belgian endive, diced
5 mushrooms, sliced
2 yellow squash, diced
2 oz. mineral bouillon
1 tablespoon sesame butter
½ bunch mint leaves, chopped
½ teaspoon ginger powder
juice of 1 lemon
olive oil
water

Preheat oven at 450° for 10 minutes. In a small bowl, make a stock of mineral bouillon, 3 oz. water, and 2 oz. olive oil. Arrange eggplant slices in a roasting pan and pour stock over them. Reduce oven to 375°, cover pan, and bake eggplant for 8 minutes. While the eggplant is cooking, sauté together briefly the olives, 2 oz. olive oil, and 3 oz. water. After a few minutes, add the spinach and escarole and cook for 3 minutes over medium heat. Put greens and olives into a bowl (be sure to save the stock), and add sesame butter, lemon juice, mint, and ginger. Set this aside while you sauté the zucchini, endive, mushrooms, and squash for 5 to 7 minutes in 2 oz. of the stock left from sautéeing the greens. When done, blend in your blender—not too smoothly! Mix the blended zucchini mixture with about a quarter of the greens.

Remove eggplants from the oven and put a slice of tomato on each eggplant slice. Top this with the remaining three-quarters of the greens. Roll each eggplant slice around some of the greens mixture. Spoon the blended vegetable mixture over the top of your eggplant rolls and serve.

EGGPLANT SUNSHINE

Gather together these ingredients:

3 eggplants, peeled
1 lb. asparagus
¼ lb. mushrooms
3 stalks celery, chopped
½ bunch parsley, chopped
1 red onion, chopped
2 large tomatoes
juice of 2 lemons
2 oz. mineral bouillon
1 tablespoon mineral powder
4 cloves garlic, minced
2 to 4 cloves garlic, chopped
1½ tablespoons sesame tahini
½ bunch sweet basil, chopped
1 teaspoon lemon thyme
olive oil
water

Preheat oven at 450° for 10 minutes. Cut each eggplant into 4 horizontal slices. Put slices into a baking pan, and pour over them a stock of mineral bouillon, mineral powder, 2 oz. olive oil, and 1½ oz. water. Reduce oven to

375°. Cover pan and bake for 8 to 10 minutes.

While the eggplant is cooking, prepare the asparagus: Chop off each asparagus tip, leaving a 1-inch stem. Coarsely chop the remaining stalks. Then sauté all the asparagus with the mushrooms in a stock of lemon juice, ½ oz. water, and 1 oz. olive oil for about 5 to 7 minutes. Watch closely as you don't want to overcook the delicate asparagus.

Remove eggplant slices from oven and drain off some of the stock for use in a tomato sauce. Set it aside in a small bowl. Sprinkle chopped garlic—as much as you'd like—over eggplant slices. Turn oven to broil, and broil eggplant and garlic for 2 to 3 minutes.

Prepare a fresh tomato sauce: in an open skillet place the stock you've saved from the baked eggplant with minced garlic, celery, parsley, and red onion. Sauté for 3 minutes; then add tomatoes (hand-squeezed). Continue cooking the sauce for 5 to 8 minutes. Add sesame tahini, sweet basil, and lemon thyme. Stir well and cook for 1 minute.

Now, you should have a pan of savory fresh tomato sauce, a pan of asparagus and mushrooms, and a roasting pan with tender eggplant slices sprinkled with garlic. Lay half of the eggplant slices flat on a serving platter. Add cooked asparagus and mushrooms. Cover with remaining slices of eggplant and top with fresh tomato sauce. Serve.

LEEKS AND EGGPLANTS

Gather together these ingredients:

8 leeks
1 eggplant, peeled
3 large zucchini, sliced
2 tomatoes, sliced
1 lb. peas
3 shallots, chopped
2 chives, chopped
½ bunch mint leaves, chopped
1 cube soya butter
olive oil
water

Preheat oven at 450° for 10 minutes. Prepare the leeks by removing and discarding the upper half of the stem, cutting off the cap (or end), and then removing the three outer layers of peel. Starting two inches from the bottom of the stem, cut the leeks into thin strips. Set aside while you cut the eggplant in half horizontally and then slice into thin strips. Place these strips in a roasting pan and cover with leeks, zucchini, and tomatoes. Make a stock of 1 cube soya butter, 1 oz. olive oil, and 1 oz. water. Pour over vegetables. Reduce oven to 350° and bake covered for 8 to 10 minutes. At the last three minutes of cooking time, add peas, shallots, chives, and mint leaves. Remove from oven and serve on a large platter. Trimming the leeks in this fashion reproduces the original leek shape in the smaller, edible, tender portion of the leek.

LIMA BEAN DELIGHT

Gather together these ingredients:

3 lbs. lima beans
½ lb. asparagus
3 red onions, finely chopped
2 Irish potatoes
3 bunches spinach
3 cloves garlic, finely chopped
¼ bunch parsley, finely chopped
¼ lb. mushrooms
3 tablespoons mineral powder
1 tablespoon sesame butter
2 stalks celery, finely chopped
2 oz. mineral bouillon
1 teaspoon balanced protein seasoning
1 teaspoon kelp
½ cube soya butter

Preheat oven at 450° for 10 minutes. Bake potatoes wrapped in tinfoil for 25 minutes at 450°. Steam the lima beans in a covered pan with mineral powder, 2 oz. olive oil, and 8 oz. water for 3 to 5 minutes. Sauté asparagus stalks and onions with a little water for 5 minutes.

Steam spinach in 4 oz. water for 3 minutes. Drain, chop fine, and add 2 garlic cloves, parsley, and sesame butter. Mix very well to a smooth, creamy texture. Set aside while you make a raw mushroom sauce: in your blender, combine the mushrooms, 1 garlic clove, celery, mineral bouillon, and 1 oz. olive oil. Remove potatoes from oven and mash (leave the skins on) with balanced protein seasoning, kelp, and soya butter.

You now should have 5 different

pans or bowls of food. Here's the delight: making a melody from a collection of notes. Mix the lima beans with the mashed potatoes and place in the center of a large serving platter. Surround these with the asparagus and onions. Top the beans and potatoes with the raw mushroom sauce and top the asparagus with the spinach-sesame cream. Serve.

OKRA STEAMED WITH SWEET POTATOES

Gather together these ingredients:

1½ lbs. okra
5 green onions, chopped
2 sweet potatoes
1 lb. peas
½ cube soya butter
1 tablespoon mineral bouillon
1 teaspoon balanced protein seasoning
olive oil
water

Preheat oven at 450° for 10 minutes. Wrap sweet potatoes in tinfoil and bake for 20 to 25 minutes. While sweet potatoes are baking, cut off and discard the woody stems and tips from the okra. Place the okra in a covered pot with 2 oz. water, 2 oz. olive oil, mineral bouillon, and green onions. Cook for 7 to 9 minutes over a low flame.

Take the potatoes from the oven and carefully remove the skins. Chop the skins well and add them to the cooked okra. Mash the sweet insides of the potatoes with soya butter and balanced protein seasoning; then mix in the raw peas. Design the potato-pea mixture to give the impression of a flat, thick, round loaf of bread. Then top this "loaf" with cooked okra, and serve.

PARSNIPS IN LENTILS

Gather together these ingredients:

6 parsnips
4 bunches spinach
1 bunch chicory
½ red onion, chopped
1½ cups lentils
2 small white onions, coarsely chopped
5 shallots, coarsely chopped
¼ lb. walnuts, finely chopped or ground
3 oz. mineral bouillon
2 tablespoons sesame butter
½ bunch mint leaves
1 tablespoon mineral powder
olive oil
water

Add lentils to 3 cups boiling water, cover and lower flame. After 10 minutes add white onions, shallots, and mineral powder. Continue to cook, covered, for 20 to 30 minutes. During the last 3 minutes, add mint leaves. While lentils are cooking, trim parsnips, then thickly slice in pointed pieces (Oriental fashion). Sauté in an open skillet for 3 to 5 minutes with 1 oz. mineral bouillon and 2 oz. olive oil.

Boil a stock of 2 oz. mineral bouillon, 2 oz. olive oil, and ½ oz. water. Add spinach and chicory and steam for about 3 minutes. When vegetables are cooked, add red onion and sesame butter; mix well. Take a flat serving platter and make a bed of cooked lentils; sprinkle walnuts over this, cover with cooked vegetables, and top with parsnips. Serve.

STUFFED RED PEPPERS

Gather together these ingredients:

8 large red bell peppers
2 onions, quartered
1 bunch broccoli
1 lb. peas
6 zucchini, diced
1 head escarole, chopped
1 bunch spinach, chopped
1 tablespoon miso
1 teaspoon mineral powder
2 cloves garlic
1 tablespoon cashew butter
juice from 1½ lemons
olive oil
water

Preheat oven at 450° for 10 minutes. Cut off the tops and clean out the seeds of the peppers. Place the pepper shells in a roasting pan with miso, mineral powder, onions, juice of 1 lemon, 2 oz. olive oil, and 3 oz. water. Reduce oven to 350° and bake peppers, covered, for 8 to 10 minutes. Meanwhile, sauté broccoli flowers (whole) and ends (chopped fine), with peas and zucchini in 3 oz. olive oil and 1 oz. water for 3 minutes. Steam, in a covered pan, escarole and spinach with 2 oz. water for 3 minutes. Toss in a couple of cloves of garlic, too.

When escarole and spinach are steamed, drain well, and add cashew butter, juice of ½ lemon, and 1 teaspoon olive oil. Remove the peppers from the oven. Blend in your blender some of the pepper stock with one quarter of the broccoli-peas-zucchini mixture and stuff the peppers about three-quarters full with this. Top with the spinach-escarole mixture. Place the peppers on a serving platter and surround them with the remainder of the cooked vegetables and the chopped greens. Serve.

RED PEPPERS AND KIDNEY BEANS

Gather together these ingredients:

2 cups dried kidney beans
8 red bell peppers
15 mushrooms, finely chopped
1 lb. peas
3 stalks celery, finely chopped
1 bunch garden cress, finely chopped
½ bunch sweet basil, finely chopped
3 tablespoons mineral powder
2 oz. mineral bouillon
1 teaspoon balanced protein seasoning
olive oil
water

Soak kidney beans for 2 days in water to cover; drain and cover with fresh water two or three times a day. After about 48 hours, drain then rinse beans in cool water. In a large pot, bring about 2 quarts of water to a full boil. Add balanced protein seasoning, 1 tablespoon mineral powder, and beans; cook over a low flame for 20 to 30 minutes.

Preheat oven at 450° for 10 minutes. Cut off the tops and clean out the seeds of the peppers. Place the pepper shells in a roasting pan with mineral bouillon, 2 tablespoons mineral powder, 2 oz. olive oil, and 3 oz. water. Reduce oven to 350° and bake peppers covered for 8 to 10 minutes.

Meanwhile, mix together the peas with the chopped mushrooms, garden cress, basil, and celery. Drain beans, saving the liquid, and place them and the vegetables together in a mixing bowl. Combine well: then blend in the blender enough of the bean-vegetable mix to stuff the peppers, using the bean juice to help provide a pleasing consistency. Remove the peppers from the oven, stuff with the blended bean-vegetable mixture, and place in the center of a serving platter. Surround them with the remaining unblended bean-vegetable mixture. Serve.

CHOPPED STRINGBEANS

Gather together these ingredients:

3 lbs. stringbeans, chopped into ¼-inch pieces
10 carrots, diced
5 beets, diced
3 cucumbers, diced
3 Belgian endives
3 leeks
2 parsnips
5 shallots, chopped (optional)
½ tablespoon miso (see section on purées)
¼ lb. pecans, shelled
juice of 2 lemons
1 oz. mineral bouillon
olive oil
water

Preheat oven at 450° for 10 minutes. Sauté stringbeans in your wok with mineral bouillon, 1 oz. olive oil, miso and 2 oz. water. Cook for only 6 to 8 minutes, stirring constantly. Remove beans from wok, and using the same stock, sauté carrots, beets, and cucumbers, adding 1 oz. olive oil and 1 oz. water. Cook these for about 5 to 7 minutes.

Cut endives, leeks, and parsnips in long thin slices and place in a roasting pan. Cover with a stock of lemon juice, shallots, and 2 oz. water. Reduce oven to 350° and bake, covered, for 7 minutes. Mix together the stringbeans, beets, carrots, and cucumbers with the pecans. Place this vegetable-nut mix on a serving dish and surround with baked endives, leeks, and parsnips. Serve.

Chapter Seven

Companion Dishes

ARTICHOKES

Gather together these ingredients:

6 artichokes
3 white onions, quartered
2 lbs. peas
5 large carrots, finely chopped
2 tablespoons mineral powder
1 oz. mineral bouillon
olive oil
water

Preheat oven at 450° for 10 minutes. Cut tips and stems from artichokes; remove the outer 2 rows of leaves and quarter artichokes. Put them in a covered roasting pan with onions, mineral powder, mineral bouillon, 3 oz. water, and 1 oz. olive oil. Reduce oven to 300° and bake artichokes for 15 to 20 minutes. Add peas and carrots and continue cooking for another 5 minutes. Serve on a large platter.

The cooking times here are approximate. You may wish to cook the artichokes slightly longer before adding vegetables.

ASPARAGUS FLAVORED

Gather together these ingredients:

1½ lbs. asparagus
1 Belgian endive, chopped
1 small avocado, chopped
juice of 2 lemons
1 teaspoon kelp
1 teaspoon mineral powder
1 teaspoon balanced protein seasoning
olive oil
water

Cut off and discard the woody ends of the asparagus; steam the tender bud ends in a covered skillet with kelp, mineral powder, balanced protein seasoning, 1 oz. olive oil, and 2 oz. water for 10 to 12 minutes. When cooked, put asparagus in a serving bowl and top with endive and avocado. Add lemon juice, 2 oz. olive oil, and stock. Serve.

ASPARAGUS AND MUSHROOM SAUCE

Gather together these ingredients:

1½ lbs. asparagus
1½ lbs. mushrooms
1 bunch parsley, chopped
2 stalks celery, chopped
2 cloves garlic, chopped
3 oz. mineral bouillon
olive oil
water

Cut asparagus stalks in half; sauté bottom halves in 2 oz. olive oil, 1 oz. water, and 1 oz. mineral bouillon for 10 to 12 minutes. Drain stock into a small bowl and blend sautéed asparagus ends in blender. Combine in a small mixing bowl the mushrooms, parsley, celery, garlic, 2 oz. mineral bouillon, 2 oz. olive oil, and the stock from the sautéed asparagus ends. Combine with asparagus ends in blender and blend into a creamy thick sauce. Place asparagus tips on a serving platter and cover with the mushroom-asparagus sauce. Broil for 3 to 5 minutes. Serve.

ASPARAGUS IN A NUT BUTTER

Gather together these ingredients:

1½ lbs. asparagus
juice of 3 lemons
1 tablespoon cashew butter
1 tablespoon almond butter
1 teaspoon miso
½ bunch garden cress, finely chopped
1 tablespoon mineral powder

Trim off and discard woody ends from asparagus. Steam the asparagus stalks in a stock of 2 oz. water, juice of 2 lemons, and mineral powder for 5 to 8 minutes. Mix together both nut butters with the juice of 1 lemon, miso, and garden cress. When asparagus is tender, add the stock to the nut butter preparation and mix until loose and fluffy. Top the asparagus with the nut butter preparation and serve.

BEANS ARE FUN

Gather together these ingredients:

1 lb. pole beans
1 lb. French beans
1 lb. yellow beans
4 cloves garlic, chopped
¼ bunch parsley, minced
¼ bunch garden cress, chopped
¼ lb. black olives, chopped
4 tomatoes, chopped
juice of 2 lemons
3 cucumbers, diced
1 tablespoon mineral powder
1 teaspoon fennel seeds
1 tablespoon cashew butter
olive oil
water

Steam beans together in a large covered pot with 8 oz. water, lemon juice, and mineral powder. While the beans are cooking—about 5 to 8 minutes—prepare a fresh tomato sauce: sauté garlic, parsley, garden cress, olives, and fennel seeds for about 3 minutes; then add tomatoes. Simmer all this for 5 to 8 minutes. Place beans on a large round serving platter and cover with one half the tomato sauce; mix well. Then mix the other half of the tomato sauce with the cashew butter and cucumbers. Spread over beans and plain tomato sauce, and serve.

BROCCOLI FOR FLAVOR

Gather together these ingredients:

6 heads broccoli
3 lemons
½ bunch mint leaves
10 mushrooms, chopped
3 cloves garlic, chopped
2 tablespoons blended almonds
1 teaspoon kelp
olive oil
water

Slice broccoli in long thin pieces, from flower to stem. Steam for 6 to 8 minutes in a covered pot with a stock of 4 oz. water, juice of 2 lemons, and mint leaves. Place broccoli in a serving bowl and add chopped garlic (use more or less, to taste), juice of 1 lemon, mushrooms, 2 oz. olive oil, and kelp. Sprinkle with blended almonds. Serve.

BROCCOLI IN RED BEET SAUCE

Gather together these ingredients:

4 bunches broccoli
10 small potatoes
3 small beets
½ bunch sweet basil
1 tablespoon mineral powder
1 tablespoon balanced protein seasoning
1 teaspoon sage
1 teaspoon oregano
olive oil
water

Preheat oven at 450° for 10 minutes. Slice off and discard woody ends of broccoli. But broccoli and potatoes in roasting pan with mineral powder, 1 oz. olive oil, and 3 oz. water. Reduce oven to 350° and bake covered for 6 to 10 minutes. Meanwhile, boil beets for 10 minutes in balanced protein seasoning and 2 oz. water. Cut cooked beets into quarters and blend in your blender with sweet basil, sage, oregano, and 1 oz. olive oil. Remove broccoli and potatoes from oven and add stock to beet mixture. Put broccoli and potatoes on serving platter, top with beet dressing, and serve.

BROCCOLI AND TOMATO

Gather together these ingredients:

2 bunches broccoli
1 red onion, chopped fine
3 tomatoes
5 cloves garlic, minced
1 oz. mineral bouillon
1 teaspoon savory
½ teaspoon fennel seeds
½ cube soya butter
olive oil

Cut off stems of broccoli and chop them. Sauté broccoli stems, garlic, and onion in 2 oz. olive oil with mineral bouillon. After 5 minutes, add broccoli flowers and tomatoes (hand-squeezed). Cover pan and continue to cook for 5 to 7 minutes. Remove cover and add savory and fennel. Cook for 5 more minutes uncovered, then add soya butter, let melt, and mix well. Serve.

BRUSSELS SPROUTS

Gather together these ingredients:

2 lbs. Brussels sprouts
1 lb. mushrooms, chopped
3 cloves garlic, whole
juice of 4 lemons
1 Belgian endive, chopped
1 cucumber, chopped
1 teaspoon oregano
olive oil

In your wok, sauté trimmed Brussels sprouts (cut stems and remove any blemished leaves), mushrooms, and garlic in 3 oz. olive oil and the juice of 3 lemons. Cover wok while sautéeing but stir frequently; cooking should take 5 to 8 minutes. Meanwhile, mix endive, cucumber, oregano, 1 oz. olive oil, and the juice from the remaining lemon. Put sautéed Brussels sprouts and mushrooms in a serving dish and top with endive mixture; serve.

THE CABBAGE WHOLE

Gather together these ingredients:

2 heads cabbage
1 bunch spinach, chopped
2 Belgian endives, chopped
¼ lb. pecans, shelled
¼ lb. black olives
1 white onion, finely chopped
2 teaspoons mineral bouillon
olive oil
water

Preheat oven at 450° for 10 minutes. Mix together spinach, endives, pecans, and olives with 2 oz. olive oil. Cut a hole vertically halfway through each cabbage. The diameter of each hole should be about one-half the size of the cabbage.

Reduce oven to 350°.

Bake the cabbages, with their caps (center pieces) in place for 5 to 8 minutes in a covered roasting pan with the onion, mineral bouillon, and 2 oz. water. Remove cabbages, remove caps, and fill each cabbage about three-quarters full with the spinach-endive mixture. Recap. Reduce oven to 300° and bake for 3 to 5 minutes in the same stock. Serve.

LIGHT CABBAGE

Gather together these ingredients:

4 stalks celery, chopped
4 shallots, chopped
2 cucumbers, chopped

2 medium red cabbage, shredded
¼ lb. raisins
2 tablespoons mineral powder
2 teaspoons kelp
½ cube soya butter
olive oil
water

Sauté celery, shallots, and cucumbers in a covered skillet with 1 oz. olive oil, 2 oz. water, and 1 tablespoon mineral powder for 5 minutes. Then add shredded cabbage and raisins. Cover pan and cook for about 3 to 6 minutes. Remove from heat, place vegetables on a serving platter, and kelp, 1 tablespoon mineral powder, and soya butter. When the soya butter melts, mix, and serve.

CARROTS

Gather together these ingredients:

12 carrots
4 zucchini, chopped
2 yellow squash, chopped
2 tomatoes, chopped
1 cucumber, chopped
1 Belgian endive, sliced thin
4 shallots, chopped
2 chives, chopped
4 crepes (see section on grains)
½ bunch garden cress
1 tablespoon mineral powder
1 teaspoon sage
½ teaspoon ginger powder
1 cube soya butter
olive oil
water

Preheat oven at 450° for 10 minutes. Slice each carrot lengthwise into 3 pieces. Put carrot pieces in baking pan with 3 oz. water, 2 oz. olive oil, and mineral powder. Reduce oven to 300° and bake covered for 8 to 10 minutes. In an open skillet, make a vegetable sauce of zucchini, yellow squash, tomatoes, 2 oz. olive oil, sage, ginger powder, and soya butter. Cook for 5 to 8 minutes. Dice crepes. Remove carrots from oven; mix diced crepes with carrots and spread on serving platter. Pour vegetable sauce over carrots and crepes and top with cucumber, endive, shallots, chives, and garden cress. Serve.

CARROTS LIGHTLY

Gather together these ingredients:

10 carrots, sliced
¼ lb. raisins
juice of 1 lemon
¼ bunch parsley, chopped
¼ bunch sweet basil, chopped
2 tablespoons mineral powder
1 teaspoon cashew butter
1 teaspoon almond butter
water

Sauté carrots in 2 oz. water and mineral powder in a covered pan 5 to 8 minutes. Mix together nut butters and add lemon juice, parsley, and sweet basil. Remove carrots from heat, add raisins, and mix well. Add nut butter mixture, mix again, and serve.

CAULIFLOWER IN BROWN POTATOES

Gather together these ingredients:

2 heads cauliflower, chopped
1 lb. peas
4 large Irish potatoes
1 large red onion, thinly sliced
2 cloves garlic, minced
½ bunch parsley, chopped
1 tablespoon miso
4 tablespoons mineral bouillon
1 teaspoon kelp
olive oil
water

In your wok, sauté cauliflower and peas in 2 oz. olive oil and 1 oz. water for about 6 to 8 minutes. Slice potatoes into flat pointed pieces. Sauté potatoes and onion in your skillet with 3 oz. olive oil, 1 oz. water, and 4 tablespoons mineral bouillon. When cooked—about 8 to 10 minutes, depending on the thickness of the potato slices—add miso, kelp, garlic, and parsley and stir well. Add cauliflower and peas to miso-potato mixture, and serve.

CAULIFLOWER AND MUSHROOMS IN TOMATO SAUCE

Gather together these ingredients:

1 head cauliflower, chopped
5 shallots, chopped
3 cloves garlic, chopped
½ bunch of fresh parsley, chopped
¼ lb. mushrooms, chopped
3 tomatoes
⅛ bulb anise, chopped
1 oz. mineral bouillon
1 tablespoon mineral powder
olive oil

Sauté cauliflower, shallots, garlic, and parsley in 2 oz. olive oil in a covered skillet for 5 minutes. Add mineral bouillon, mushrooms, tomatoes (hand-squeezed), anise, and mineral powder. Cook for 5 to 8 minutes. Serve.

CAULIFLOWER TO TASTE

Gather together these ingredients:

2 large heads cauliflower, cubed
6 zucchini, chopped
6 cloves garlic, minced
1 head escarole, chopped
2 tomatoes, sliced
¼ lb. cashew pieces
juice of 2 lemons
½ bunch sweet basil
1 teaspoon mineral powder
olive oil

Sauté cauliflower, zucchini, and garlic in 3 oz. olive oil for 5 to 7 minutes, stirring continuously. In the last 3 minutes of cooking, add the chopped escarole. When cooked, place vegetables in serving bowl and add lemon juice, basil, cashew pieces, mineral powder. Top with sliced tomatoes; serve.

A FLAVOR OF EGGPLANT

Gather together these ingredients:

4 eggplants, peeled
1 Belgian endive, chopped
1 bunch parsley, minced
½ small onion, chopped
2 shallots, chopped
1 lb. peas
2 oz. mineral bouillon
juice of 1 lemon
olive oil
water

Preheat oven at 450° for 10 minutes. Quarter eggplants, then slice into thin pointed slices (Oriental fashion). Make a stock in your roasting pan of mineral bouillon, lemon juice, 2 oz. olive oil, and 3 oz. water. Add eggplant slices, reduce oven to 350°, and bake covered for 8 to 10 minutes. Mix together Belgian endive, parsley, onion, shallots, and peas. When eggplants are cooked, remove from oven, toss with endive mixture, and serve.

EGGPLANT IN MUSHROOM SAUCE

Gather together these ingredients:

3 eggplants, peeled and sliced
½ lb. mushrooms, sliced
2 stalks celery, coarsely chopped
¼ bunch parsley, chopped
2 cloves garlic, minced
1 teaspoon cashew butter
3 oz. mineral bouillon
1 teaspoon kelp
olive oil
water

Preheat broiler for 5 minutes. In your roasting pan put sliced eggplant with kelp, 2 oz. mineral bouillon, 2 oz. olive oil, and 3 oz. water. Broil for 10 to 12 minutes. Meanwhile, blend in your blender the mushrooms with celery, parsley, garlic, cashew butter, 1 oz. mineral bouillon, and 2 oz. olive oil. Check on the eggplant and when the slices are slightly brown, remove pan from oven. Spoon mushroom sauce over slices, turn them over, add a little more sauce, and, if you'd like, put pan under broiler for another 3 to 5 minutes. Serve.

CHOPPED EGGPLANTS WITH PEAS

Gather together these ingredients:

3 eggplants, cubed
1 lb. peas
½ bunch sweet basil
1 sweet potato, thinly sliced
½ cube soya butter
1 teaspoon nutritional yeast

Preheat oven at 450° for 10 minutes. Put cubed eggplants in a covered roasting pan; reduce oven to 350° and bake eggplants for 10 minutes. Then open baking pan and add peas and basil, cover again and bake for another 3 to 5 minutes. While this is cooking, sauté sweet potato in soya butter. Remove eggplants and peas from oven, spoon into serving dish, top with sautéed sweet potato, and sprinkle with nutritional yeast. Serve.

LEEKS

Gather together these ingredients:

8 leeks
2 tablespoons sesame tahini
½ cup sesame seeds
1 tomato, thinly sliced
1 avocado, thinly sliced
olive oil
water

Preheat oven at 450° for 15 minutes. Prepare the leeks by removing and discarding the upper half of the stem, cutting off the cap (or end), and then removing the three outer layers of peel. Starting 2 inches from the bottom of the stem, cut the leeks into thin strips. Put leeks in a covered roasting pan with sesame tahini, sesame seeds, 2 oz. water, and 2 oz. olive oil. Reduce oven to 350° and bake for 5 to 8 minutes. When leeks are done, place them on a serving platter and top with thin slices of tomato and avocado. Serve.

This method for trimming the leeks actually reproduces the original leek shape in the smaller, edible, tender portion of the leek.

OKRA, A LIGHT DISH

Gather together these ingredients:

1½ lbs. okra
2 Belgian endives, chopped
8 mushrooms, chopped
1 cucumber, chopped
¼ lb. Greek olives
1 teaspoon cashew butter
juice of 2 lemons
3 chives, finely chopped
olive oil
water

Preheat oven at 450° for 10 minutes. Cut off and discard the hard ends and tips of okra. Put okra in a roasting pan with 2 oz. olive oil and 1 oz. water. Reduce oven to 350° and bake covered for 6 to 8 minutes. When cooked, add cashew butter. Mix together Belgian endives, mushrooms, cucumber, and olives with fresh lemon juice, chives, and 1 oz. olive oil. Add this mixture to cooked okra, and serve.

PARSNIPS EASY

Gather together these ingredients:

6 parsnips
2 tomatoes
3 cloves garlic
¼ bunch parsley, chopped
10 black olives, pitted and chopped
3 green bell peppers, chopped
3 yellow squash, chopped
½ bulb anise
1 cube safflower butter
olive oil
water

Preheat oven at 450° for 10 minutes. Trim stems and tips from parsnips; put parsnips, whole, in a covered roasting pan with tomatoes (hand-squeezed), garlic, parsley, olives, 2 oz. olive oil, and 1 oz. water. Reduce oven to 350° and bake for 10 to 12 minutes. While parsnips are cooking sauté peppers, anise, and squash in 2 oz. water and safflower butter. Use an uncovered skillet, stir frequently, and cook for about 5 to 8 minutes. Remove parsnips from oven and mix parsnips and stock with sautéed vegetables. Serve.

PEPPERS AND POTATOES

Gather together these ingredients:

5 red bell peppers
3 green bell peppers
3 green onions
3 shallots (optional)
¼ lb. mushrooms
1 cucumber, peeled
6 small russet potatoes, sliced
2 white onions, sliced
¼ lb. black olives, sliced
1 chili pepper, whole
1 oz. mineral bouillon
½ cube soya butter
olive oil
water

Chop peppers, green onions, shallots, mushrooms, and cucumber in pointed pieces (Oriental fashion); then sauté in mineral bouillon, 2 oz. olive oil, and 3 oz. water for about 5 minutes. When cooked, drain stock into skillet containing potatoes, white onions, black olives, and chili pepper. Sauté for 5 to 8 minutes. Keep skillet covered except to stir frequently, so that vegetables will cook evenly and without sticking. When tender, add soya butter, allow to melt, and mix well. Add potato mixture to peppers, and serve.

COLORFUL PEPPERS

Gather together these ingredients:

5 red bell peppers
3 green bell peppers
1 red onion
4 yellow squash
1 teaspoon nutritional yeast
½ cube soya butter
1 teaspoon mineral powder
olive oil
water

Chop peppers, onion, and squash in pointed pieces (Oriental fashion). Sauté for 5 to 8 minutes in a stock of 3 oz. water and 2 oz. olive oil. When tender, add soya butter and mineral powder, mix well, sprinkle with yeast, and serve.

Chapter Eight

The Italian In Me

"Grandma, how come you always make me eat?"

"Johnny boy, itsa gooda for you, it make you healthy."

"But Grandma, I'm going to get fat if I eat like this."

"You no geta fat. Exercise and enjoy the wonderful, the delicious food from the Old Country."

Typically, my grandmother knew best. She was a beautiful Italian princess whose hand of gold and warm heart filled many a person with joy. Always she was baking cookies, or making pizza with spinach and mushrooms, or serving peach, pear, or apple cordials the she brewed herself in the cellar. Holidays were a feast. Thirty to forty screaming Italians seated at two tables—one for the kids, one for the grown-ups. As the oldest grandson and having lost my mother, I was always seated next to my grandfather, my best friend and my most admired eater. We had a great rapport. I would always tease, "How many dishes of spaghetti have you eaten in your life?" He would laugh and gesture with his hands as if the number was beyond calculation. I can hear Grandma now scolding Grandpa for getting me drunk on homemade wine as a kid.

And the food! How I remember the spaghetti with fresh tomato sauce, sweet basil, garlic, and black olives; and after eating, the rhythmic tune of Grandpa playing the trombone while I danced.

The food of my Italian heritage is closely linked with some of the most profound experiences of my life. As we four played our symphony to the slurping sounds of spaghetti, I learned what human tenderness and frailty is.

I have combined into my world of vegetables some of the best Old World dishes that Grandma ever produced. In all my recipes, I carefully lay out what ingredients to gather before you begin a recipe. I suggest how much of each ingredient to use, down to the smallest portion of a teaspoon. Grandma never cooked that way; she was an intuitive cook—it was always add a little of this, or a pinch of that, plus a handful of those nice greens we saw at the store this morning. She never said to cook a dish for 5 minutes, or for half an hour; instead she listened to the symphony of the foods. Listen to your food; it will tell you when it has been cooked enough.

SPAGHETTI

Gather together these ingredients:

1 lb. dry spaghetti
olive oil
water

Bring 8 cups of water to a rolling boil. Add 1 tablespoon olive oil and spaghetti. Cook for 10 to 12 minutes. Drain in a colander and add sauce of your choice. Serve.

Cooking time depends on your preference for spaghetti texture. The Italians say *al dente,* spaghetti on the chewy side; some prefer spaghetti a little softer. Oil is added to the water to prevent the spaghetti from sticking.

Gracing the kitchen of the Natural Chef is spaghetti and macaroni of many varieties—buckwheat, sesame, artichoke, spinach, and soya.

PIZZA ALLA GRANDMA

Gather together these ingredients:

5 cups whole wheat pastry flour
1 tablespoon honey (optional)
6 large tomatoes
5 cloves garlic, minced
1 stalk celery, finely chopped
1 bunch parsley, chopped
10 shallots, halved (optional)
1 red onion, finely chopped
1 teaspoon peppermint
1 teaspoon spearmint
1 teaspoon fennel seeds
½ bunch sweet basil (optional)
½ lb. mushrooms, chopped
1 bunch spinach, chopped
1 lb. tofu, drained
1 teaspoon mineral bouillon
1 teaspoon mineral powder
½ teaspoon miso
olive oil
water

Preheat a griddle to 450°. Make a *thick* mixture of flour, 2 to 3 cups of water, and honey (optional). Lower griddle to 350°, pour 1 tablespoon of olive oil on griddle, and wipe off immediately with a paper towel. Using a ladle, spoon batter onto the grill as if making a very thick pancake. Cook till brown on one side, turn, and cook on the other side. Remove from heat, and set aside in a warm place.

Make a tomato sauce: sauté the garlic, celery, ½ bunch parsley, shallots, and onions in 2 oz. olive oil and 1 oz. water for 2 to 3 minutes. Then add tomatoes (hand-squeezed) and cook uncovered over a low flame for 5 to 8 minutes. Add peppermint, spearmint, and fennel seeds and cook another 2 to 3 minutes. If it's in season, add fresh basil.

In a separate skillet sauté mushrooms with mineral powder, 2 oz. olive oil, and 1 oz. water for 5 to 8 minutes. Add spinach and stir; cover and lower flame. Cook for 2 minutes, then drain stock into a small bowl and set aside. Chop spinach in pan. Mash tofu well with the rest of the parsley. Sauté this in the mushroom-spinach stock adding 2 oz. olive oil, miso, mineral bouillon, and about 4 oz. of the tomato sauce. Stir constantly: this should be fluffy and thick, not watery.

Mix tofu sauce with mushroom-spinach mixture; put all this on one half of your pizza base and fold over. Cover with the tomato sauce.

IMPROVISATIONS: Blend tomato sauce with ½ bunch chopped steamed chicory and ½ bunch chopped steamed escarole to make a red and green sauce. Or, add sliced olives to tomato sauce.

VEGI MEATA BALLS

Gather together these ingredients:

3 potatoes (1 sweet, 1 yam, 1 of your choice)
1 bunch spinach
4 cloves garlic
¼ cube safflower butter
10 mushrooms, chopped
¼ bunch parsley
¼ bunch escarole, chopped
2 shallots, chopped (optional)
2 beets, finely chopped
olive oil
water

Preheat oven at 450° for 10 minutes. Wrap each potato in tinfoil; reduce oven to 350° and bake potatoes for 20 to 25 minutes. While they're cooking, sauté in a covered skillet the spinach and garlic, in 2 oz. olive oil and 1 oz. water for 3 minutes. Drain well, saving the stock. Finely chop cooked spinach and garlic.

Remove the three potatoes from the oven, mash well together, and add safflower butter. Mix in the sautéed chopped spinach and garlic. Use the stock from the spinach in which to sauté the mushrooms, shallots, and beets. Cook for 3 to 5 minutes and then add escarole and parsley; cook for another 3 minutes. If you need more liquid, add a little olive oil. Drain and add to baked mashed potatoes and spinach; mix well. You can add a little of the mushroom stock but not too much as it will make the potatoes soggy. Roll mixture into vegi meata balls. If desired, broil for 3 to 5 minutes.

RIGATONI IN GREENS

Gather together these ingredients:

1 lb. rigatoni
1 red onion, minced
½ small head cabbage, finely chopped
1 stalk celery, minced
½ lb. tofu, drained
3 carrots, diced
3 tomatoes
1 bunch spinach, chopped
1 bunch chicory, chopped
½ bunch parsley, chopped
5 cloves garlic, chopped
1 teaspoon mineral powder
1 tablespoon mineral bouillon
1 tablespoon balanced protein seasoning
olive oil
water

Sauté for 3 minutes in a covered skillet the onion, cabbage, and celery with 1 oz. olive oil and 2 oz. water. Add a little more olive oil, 1 teaspoon mineral powder, and 1 tablespoon mineral bouillon and cook for another 3 minutes. Drain stock into a small bowl and set aside. Combine vegetables in your blender, adding tofu and 1 clove garlic. Slowly add a little stock as you blend—enough to make consistency smooth but very thick.

To a large pot of boiling water, add rigatoni and a little olive oil to prevent sticking. Cook for 12 to 15 minutes, or to the consistency you like. Drain and rinse.

In a skillet, sauté 2 chopped cloves of garlic, 2 oz. olive oil, and 1 oz. water for 2 minutes. Then add spinach and chicory; stir frequently as you cook for about 3 minutes. Add balanced protein seasoning, mix well, cover and remove from heat.

Add remaining stock to a hot skillet with 2 cloves garlic, parsley, and 1 oz. olive oil. Sauté for 2 minutes. Then add 3 tomatoes (hand-squeezed); lower flame and cook for 5 to 8 minutes.

In a large serving dish, layer: tomato sauce, rigatoni, blended vegetables and tofu, rigatoni, the rest of the tomato sauce, and top with spinach and chicory. Serve.

RAVIOLI ALLA GRANDMA

Gather together these ingredients:

6 crepes (see crepe recipe)
3 cloves garlic, chopped
1 red onion, chopped
½ lb. mushrooms, minced
½ head escarole, minced
½ bunch chicory, minced
½ lb. tofu, drained
3 tomatoes
½ cube safflower butter
5 olives (black or green), pitted and chopped
1 oz. mineral bouillon
olive oil
water

Sauté in an open skillet 2 cloves garlic, onion, mushrooms, mineral bouillon, 2 oz. olive oil, and 1 oz. water for 5 to 8 minutes. Drain and set aside, saving stock. Using that same stock, sauté 1 clove garlic and olives for 2 minutes. Add chicory and escarole and cook another 3 minutes. Drain and set aside, once again saving stock. This time put the stock in your pan and heat from 1 to 2 minutes, adding a little olive oil, if necessary. Add tomatoes (hand-squeezed) and cook for 5 to 8 minutes. Then add tofu (also hand-squeezed); mix continually for 2 minutes, adding the soya butter toward the end of the cooking time.

Take one-half of the tomato sauce and put it in your blender; add one-half of the mushrooms and one-half of the escarole-chicory mix; blend all to a creamy sauce.

Cut the sides of each round crepe so that it becomes a square ravioli. In the center, put some (you decide the quantity) of the unblended escarole-chicory and some of the sautéed mushrooms and onion; top with the blended mixture. Fold the ravioli in half and pinch the edges together with a fork. Pour the tomato sauce over your ravioli and serve.

LASAGNA ALLA ORGANIC JOHN

Gather together these ingredients:

4 lbs. fresh tomatoes
10 cloves garlic, minced
3 red onion, finely diced
5 stalks celery, chopped
1½ bunch parsley, chopped
2 slices ginger root
2 tablespoons mineral powder
½ lb. tofu, drained
1 tablespoon miso
4 oz. mineral bouillon
4 eggplants, peeled and cubed
2 lbs. zucchini, cubed
1 tablespoon arrowroot (optional)
½ bunch chives
1½ lbs. mushrooms, sliced
5 shallots, chopped fine
1½ lbs. lasagna (sesame)
1 bunch of spinach, slightly steamed (optional)
olive oil
water

Preheat oven at 450° for 10 minutes. Sauté together in a large pot: garlic, 1 red onion, ½ bunch parsley, 2 stalks celery, 2 oz. olive oil, and ½ oz. water. After 3 minutes add tomatoes (hand-squeezed), the rest of the celery and parsley, ginger root, 1 tablespoon mineral powder, and 1 oz. mineral bouillon. Cook all this on a low flame for 20 minutes. Blend in the arrowroot to make sauce thicker, if desired.

Meanwhile, put cubed eggplants in a small covered baking dish with 3 oz. water, and 2 oz. olive oil, 2 oz. mineral bouillon, and 1 tablespoon mineral powder. In another small baking dish put the cubed zucchini with 3 oz. water, 1 oz. mineral bouillon, and 2 oz. olive oil. Reduce oven to 350° and bake the zucchini and eggplant 10 to 15 minutes.

To five quarts of boiling water, add lasagna noodles and a little olive oil to prevent sticking. Cook for about 20 minutes, stirring frequently, or cook to the consistency you prefer. Drain and rinse in cool water.

Sauté in a skillet 2 red onions and mushrooms in 2 oz. olive oil and 1 oz. water for 3 to 5 minutes; during the last minute or two of cooking, add chives, ½ bunch parsley, tofu, miso, and 2 oz. olive oil. Turn off heat, and set pan aside. Remove baking eggplants and zucchini from oven.

Now, let's take all these full bowls and pans and make some Lasagna alla Organic John. Layer in a large serving dish: a little tomato sauce with 1 oz. olive oil; a thick layer of lasagna; eggplant; thin layer of lasagna; more tomato sauce; zucchini; thin layer of lasagna; more tomato sauce; mushroom-tofu comination; spinach (optional); remainder of lasagna; remainder of tomato sauce. Serve and enjoy.

Be sure to read this recipe carefully before you begin cooking as it's a little complicated.

FETTUCCINE VERDI ALLA RAIMONDO

Gather together these ingredients:

2 lbs. green fettuccine
8 mushrooms, thinly sliced
4 large tomatoes, diced
4 cloves garlic, minced
1 cup pignolia nuts
½ bunch parsley, chopped
¼ bunch sweet basil, chopped
1 cube safflower butter
olive oil
water

Add fettuccine to a large pot of boiling water with a little olive oil to prevent sticking. Cook for about 6 minutes or until tender. While fettuccine is cooking, mix together mushrooms, tomatoes, garlic, pignolia nuts, parsley, basil, and ½ cup olive oil.

When fettuccine is done, drain well, rinse briefly in cold water, and return it to pot. Add safflower butter, allow to melt, and mix well until fettuccine is coated with butter. Add sauce, mix well, and serve very hot.

ARTICHOKES ALLA COUSIN JOHN

Gather together these ingredients:

4 large artichokes
5 cloves garlic
1 large red onion, halved
1 lemon
4 tablespoons (½ cube) soya butter
kernels from 1 ear uncooked corn
1 teaspoon miso
¼ bunch basil, chopped
¼ bunch parsley, chopped
4 teaspoons mineral bouillon
1½ tablespoons almond butter
1 teaspoon balnced protein seasoning
olive oil
water

Cut tips and stems from artichokes and remove the outer two rows of leaves. Spread the artichokes open like flowers and place them in a large pot with onion halves and 1 quart water (so that artichokes are about half covered with water). Begin to heat water as you add one garlic clove, 1 teaspoon mineral bouillon, and 1 teaspoon olive oil to each artichoke. Cut lemon in half and squeeze juice onto artichokes; then drop lemon rind into the cooking water. Bring water to a boil, lower flame, and cook 10 to 15 minutes. In the last 3 minutes of cooking time, add 1 tablespoon of safflower butter to each artichoke.

When artichokes are cooked, arrange them on a serving platter. Remove the lemon rind from the cooking pot and pour the remaining stock into your blender. Add corn, miso, 1 more clove of garlic, basil, parsley, almond butter, and balanced protein seasoning. Blend together and pour over the artichokes. Serve.

IMPROVISATIONS: If basil is out of season, substitute spinach.

BEANS AND PEAS IN RED PEPPERS

Gather together these ingredients:

2 lbs. lima beans
2 lbs. peas
8 red bell peppers
2 bunches spinach
1 cube soya butter
1 teaspoon almond butter
2 tomatoes, sliced
1 teaspoon mineral powder
1 teaspoon mineral bouillon
olive oil
water

Preheat oven at 450° for 10 minutes. Steam lima beans and peas in a stock of 3 oz. water and soya butter for 3 to 5 minutes. Blend in your blender half of this mixture into a thick stock, adding mineral bouillon and a little olive oil. Set aside.

Carefully cut off tops and remove seeds and core of peppers. Reduce oven to 350°. Put peppers in covered roasting pan with mineral powder, 2 oz. water, and 1 oz. olive oil and bake for 8 minutes. When spinach is done, drain, chop fine and add almond butter.

Remove the peppers from the oven and stuff them half full with the blended beans and peas. Fill to the top with chopped spinach. Place peppers on a serving platter and surround them with the other half of the bean-pea mixture. Top each pepper with a slice of raw tomato; serve.

EGGPLANTS AND SPINACH STUFFED IN A LOAF OF BREAD

Gather together these ingredients:

2 eggplants, peeled and diced
4 scallions, finely chopped
2 bunches spinach
5 cloves garlic, chopped
1 loaf of bread, unsliced
1 tablespoon SeaZun
2 tomatoes
1 tablespoon nutritional yeast
1 tablespoon mineral powder
½ bunch parsley, chopped
1 teaspoon balanced protein seasoning
olive oil
water

Preheat oven at 450° for 10 minutes. Sauté eggplant with scallions, mineral powder, 2 oz. olive oil, and 2 oz. water for 5 to 8 minutes. Remove from heat and set aside. In a separate pan, steam spinach with 2 oz. water for about 3 minutes. Then sauté for 3 to 5 minutes the tomatoes (hand-squeezed) with 2 cloves garlic, 2 oz. olive oil, and the balanced protein seasoning. Slice the bread in half lengthwise and hollow it out a little.

Brush the insides of the bread halves with a little olive oil mixed with chopped parsley and 3 cloves of chopped garlic. Reduce oven to 350° and bake bread halves for 5 minutes on an open platter. Remove halves from oven and stuff with the eggplants and scallions, then cover with the spinach; top all with the tomato sauce. Serve open-faced or closed; sliced or whole, as you prefer.

FAVE ALLA GRANDPA

Gather together these ingredients:

3 lbs. fave beans
2 bunches broccoli rabi (Italian broccoli), chopped
½ bunch dandelion greens, finely chopped
4 green peppers, chopped
½ lb. mushrooms
3 chives, sliced
½ cube soya butter
3 bay leaves
1 teaspoon oregano
1 teaspoon lemon thyme
olive oil
water

Preheat oven at 450° for 10 minutes. Combine in your roasting pan the chives, oregano, lemon thyme, 2 oz. water, and 2 oz. olive oil. Cover pan and place in the oven for 3 to 5 minutes. Then lower oven to 300° and add fave beans. Cook for 7 to 10 minutes. Meanwhile sauté together broccoli rabi, dandelion greens, and peppers in a stock of bay leaves, 1 oz. water, and 2 oz. olive oil. Cook for 5 minutes.

In another pan, sauté the mushrooms in 1 oz. water and the soya butter. If mushrooms are small, leave them whole; otherwise slice in half. Remove fave beans from oven and place them in the center of a large serving platter. Top with the cooked mushrooms and surround with the broccoli rabi, dandelion greens, and green peppers. Serve.

MUSHROOMS UNDER A BLANKET OF CHEESE

Gather together these ingredients:

12 large mushrooms (stems removed)
½ lb. rennetless Monterey Jack cheese, grated
½ eggplant, peeled and diced
2 tomatoes
1 large red onion, minced
1 zucchini, chopped
2 cloves garlic, minced
1 teaspoon balanced protein seasoning
½ cube safflower butter
½ bunch parsley, chopped fine

Sauté for 3 minutes in an open skillet the tomatoes (hand-squeezed), onions, and 2 oz. olive oil. Add mushroom caps; cover, and continue to cook for 5 to 8 minutes over a low flame. In another skillet, sauté the chopped eggplant and zucchini, parsley, garlic, balanced protein seasoning, and safflower butter for 3 to 5 minutes. Use a medium flame and stir constantly.

Remove the sautéed mushrooms from the pan and set aside; place the remaining tomato sauce into a blender. Add the zucchini-eggplant mixture and blend well. Stuff sautéed mushroom caps with this mixture; place the extra in the center of a serving platter and arrange the stuffed mushrooms around it. Top stuffed mushrooms and vegetables with grated cheese.

IMPROVISATION: Bits of tofu can be added along with the cheese.

STUFFED MUSHROOMS WITH YESTERDAY'S BREAD

Gather together these ingredients:

12 large mushrooms (stems removed)
3 or 4 slices of leftover bread (hard or toasted)
2 or 3 cloves garlic, minced
1 bunch parsley, chopped
¼ bunch watercress, chopped
2 medium zucchini, diced
5 olives, black or green, pitted and chopped
1 oz. mineral bouillon
olive oil
water

Heat mineral bouillon, 1 oz. water, and 2 oz. olive oil in a covered skillet over a low flame. Add the mushroom caps, stem side up, put a little chopped garlic in each cap, and sauté for about 6 minutes. In your blender, blend the bread into bread crumbs. Set the crumbs aside in a small bowl.

Sauté the zucchini in 1 oz. olive oil and 2 oz. water for 3 to 5 minutes. Combine the sautéed zucchini with the olives, parsley, and watercress into a thick paste; mix in bread crumbs, and use this zucchini-bread mixture to stuff the sautéed mushroom caps. Place what remains of this mixture in the center of a serving dish and arrange the stuffed mushrooms around it.

IMPROVISATIONS: This is especially good served with sliced tomatoes lightly coated with olive oil and basil. Also, a little yeast sprinkled on the mushrooms is terrific. If you use Parmesan cheese instead, omit the mineral bouillon.

OKRA AND TOMATO SAUCE ALLA COUSIN BOY

Gather together these ingredients:

1 lb. okra
3 cloves garlic, chopped
1 red onion, finely chopped
½ bunch celery, finely chopped
2 cucumbers, sliced
3 tomatoes
olive oil
water

Sauté over a low flame the garlic, onion, celery, cucumbers, and tomatoes (hand-squeezed) with 1 oz. olive oil and 2 oz. water for 3 to 5 minutes. Cut off and discard the hard ends and tips of the okra. Add okra to sautéed vegetables, cook for another 5 to 8 minutes, and serve.

COLORFUL PEPPERS ALLA AUNT JOSIE

Gather together these ingredients:

5 red bell peppers
3 green bell peppers
4 yellow squash
1 red onion, diced
1 teaspoon nutritional yeast
1 teaspoon fennel seeds
juice of ½ lemon
½ cube soya butter
1 teaspoon mineral powder
olive oil
water

Chop peppers and squash in pointed pieces (Oriental fashion). Sauté with onions for 5 to 8 minutes in a stock of 3 oz. water and 2 oz. olive oil. When tender, add soya butter, lemon juice, fennel seeds, and mineral powder. Mix well. Sprinkle with yeast and serve.

TOMATO LIGHTLY

Gather together these ingredients:

6 large tomatoes
1 head chicory, finely chopped
4 cloves garlic: 2 minced, 2 whole
¼ lb. mushrooms, sliced
2 medium carrots, finely chopped
4 green onions, chopped
2 beets, diced
1 teaspoon mineral bouillon
1 teaspoon nutritional yeast
1 teaspoon kelp
1 teaspoon mineral powder
olive oil
water

Preheat oven at 450° for 10 minutes. Carefully cut off the tops of the tomatoes and spoon insides out into a covered roasting pan with 2 whole cloves garlic, 1 oz. mineral bouillon, 2 oz. olive oil, and 1 oz. water. Reduce oven to 300° and place tomato shells in the pan; cover and bake for 5 to 7 minutes.

While tomato shells are cooking, slightly sauté beets and carrots with green onions, kelp, mineral powder, 1 oz. water, and 2 oz. olive oil. Cook for 3 to 5 minutes; then add mushrooms, chicory, and minced garlic. Remove tomato shells from oven and stuff with this mixture. Return stuffed tomatoes to the roasting pan and bake at 300° for another 3 minutes. Lightly sprinkle with nutritional yeast before serving.

IMPROVISATION: If you wish, the stock the shells are baked in can be spooned over the tomatoes right before serving. Tomatoes are not to be seen as a complementing course, but rather as a companion dish, always in the company of another course.

SANDWICHES

As a kid in Brooklyn, I was always the envy of my neighborhood at lunchtime. We'd all sit on the curb with our lunchboxes and one by one show off the delights within. Everybody else would display soggy sandwiches, mushy fruits, or wilted celery. Ah, but my lunchbox held some of my grandmother's love: last night's dinner between two slices of homemade bread. Those lunches taught me that bread does not have to be pale and limp; it should be a solid foundation, nutritionally as well as actually, for the essence of a meal. And the filling of a sandwich does not have to be peanut butter and jelly or wilted lettuce and bologna. Try some of these: sautéed spinach and mushrooms with sliced tomatoes on homebaked sourdough bread; or Italian sourdough bread with baked eggplant; or sautéed mustard greens and tofu and black olives on black rye bread. Add a few slices of cucumbers to any of these . . . or an avocado purée.

Remember to keep sandwiches full of greens, tomatoes, eggplants—avoid the combination of starches and proteins. Put imagination and creativity between your bread slices. Tasty!

Chapter Nine

Sauces, Purées, and Spreads

In certain cuisines *sauces* are used to disguise inferior cuts of meat or to numb the palate. Though I believe a sauce should have a personality all its own, it must be neither feeble nor overbearing. My sauces have been created to enhance the natural flavors of grains, and to bring forth the delicate tastes of vegetables.

Purées made from raw or cooked vegetables add a little extra touch to foods. Hors d'oeuvres and canapes topped with natural purées are interesting, colorful, and nutritional. Exciting new sandwiches can be invented using purées. Best of all are purées over cooked vegetables, an unexpected sharing of flavors.

Spreads made from nuts are a superb source of protein, and are essential for a universal menu. Best uncooked, they are a delightful treat at any meal or afternoon snack. For those with limited eating time, a nut spread sandwich is quick, tasty, and nutritional.

With your imagination, sauces, purées, and spreads will become delightful and delicious additions to your menu.

Sauces

A sauce is the liquid result of the blending of vegetables to create a unique taste combination from myriad individual flavors. One of these best ways to serve a sauce is over spaghetti; I've included my favorite garnet, terra, and emerald sauces so you can experiment. I recommend using these sauces with noodles made with water and artichoke, buckwheat, spinach, or sesame flour. These contain no artificial coloring, preservatives, eggs, sugar, honey, or salt. The spaghetti you choose, served with one or several of these sauces, will be an entirely new gourmet experience—light, yet earthy, robust, and satisfying.

TOMATO ASPARAGUS SAUCE

Gather together these ingredients:

4 cloves garlic, minced
3 shallots, chopped
1 stalk celery, diced
4 tomatoes
1 lb. asparagus, chopped
½ cube soya butter
½ bunch sweet basil, chopped
1 teaspoon rosemary
1 teaspoon lemon thyme
olive oil
water

Sauté in a covered pan the garlic, shallots, and celery in 2 oz. olive oil and 1½ oz. water. Cook for about 5 minutes over a low flame and then add the tomatoes (hand-squeezed). Cook for another 10 minutes; add asparagus. Cook for yet 10 more minutes; add soya butter, sweet basil, rosemary, and lemon thyme.

MUSHROOM TOMATO SAUCE

Gather together these ingredients:

4 cloves garlic, minced
4 green onions, chopped
2 shallots, chopped
1 teaspoon oregano
½ lb. mushrooms, sliced
1 bunch garden cress, chopped
3 tomatoes
2 oz. mineral bouillon
¼ mint leaves, chopped
olive oil
water

Sauté in a covered pan the garlic, onions, shallots, and oregano in 2 oz. olive oil and 1½ oz. water. Cook for 5 minutes over a low flame and then add the mushrooms and garden cress. Continue to cook for another 5 minutes, still covered; then add mineral bouillon and the tomatoes (hand-squeezed). Uncover pan and cook for 10 to 15 minutes. Add mint leaves.

CARROT AND TOMATOES WITH ENDIVE SAUCE

Gather together these ingredients:

5 carrots, diced
1 Belgian endive, sliced
4 cloves garlic, minced
3 shallots, chopped
3 tomatoes
1 teaspoon mineral powder
1 teaspoon kelp
½ cube soya butter
olive oil

Sauté carrots, endive, garlic, and shallots in 2 oz. olive oil for 8 minutes in a covered pan. Add the tomatoes (hand-squeezed) and cook for another 10 minutes. Add mineral powder, kelp, and soya butter. Mix well.

TOMATO AND SESAME TAHINI SAUCE

Gather together these ingredients:

3 cloves garlic, chopped
¼ bunch parsley, minced
½ red onion, chopped
3 tomatoes
1 tablespoon mineral powder
2 tablespoons sesame tahini
olive oil

Sauté garlic, parsley, and onion in 2 oz. olive oil for 3 minutes. Add the tomatoes (hand-squeezed), and mineral powder; cook for 10 minutes. Add sesame tahini; cook for 5 more minutes.

TOMATO SAUCE

Gather together these ingredients:

4 cloves garlic, chopped
2 shallots, chopped
½ red onion, chopped
3 tomatoes
1 bunch sweet basil, chopped
1 teaspoon lemon thyme
½ cube soya butter
olive oil

Sauté garlic, shallots, and onion in 2 oz. olive oil for 3 minutes. Add the tomatoes (hand-squeezed), and cook for 10 to 15 minutes in an uncovered skillet. When cooked, add sweet basil, lemon thyme, and soya butter.

Terra Sauces

MAINLY MUSHROOMS

Combine in your blender:

½ lb. mushrooms, coarsely chopped
3 oz. mineral bouillon
¼ bunch parsley
1 clove garlic, coarsely chopped
2 oz. olive oil

MAINLY CUCUMBERS

Sauté for five minutes in a covered pan:

3 green onions, chopped
2 tablespoons miso
1 oz. mineral bouillon
1 bunch garden cress, chopped
2 cucumbers, peeled and finely chopped
1 cube soya butter
2 oz. water

MAINLY EGGPLANT

Sauté 1 eggplant (peeled and diced) for 8 minutes in 2 oz. olive oil. Then combine eggplant in your blender with:

2 oz. mineral bouillon
juice of 1 lemon
½ bunch spinach, chopped
½ tablespoon miso
1 oz. olive oil

MAINLY LEEKS

Sauté 2 leeks for 5 minutes in ½ cube soya butter and 1 oz. mineral bouillon. Combine leeks in your blender with:

1 clove garlic
1 teaspoon miso
½ bunch parsley, chopped
1 oz. mineral bouillon
juice of 2 lemons
2 oz. olive oil

Emerald Sauces

PESTO ALLA ORGANIC JOHN

Gather together these ingredients:

2 bunches parsley, minced
3 bunches sweet basil, minced
6 cloves garlic, minced
2 tomatoes
¼ lb. pignolia nuts
1 cube safflower butter
olive oil

In a blender combine the parsley, basil, 4 cloves garlic, and pignolia nuts. Sauté the remaining 2 cloves of garlic, tomatoes (hand-squeezed), and 2 oz. olive oil for 5 to 8 minutes. When cooked, add safflower butter and blended parsley-basil mix.

VARIATIONS ON A PESTO THEME

Spinach pesto

Sauté for 3 minutes:

2 cloves garlic, minced
3 shallots, chopped
½ white onion, chopped
2 oz. olive oil

Slightly steam 2 bunches of chopped spinach; combine in your blender the drained spinach, sautéed garlic, shallots, onions, and 1 teaspoon cashew butter. Blend well.

Peas pesto

Sauté for 5 minutes:

1 lb. peas
3 cloves garlic, chopped
2 green onions, chopped
2 oz. olive oil

Then combine in your blender.

Asparagus Pesto

Sauté for 5 minutes:

1 lb. asparagus, chopped
1 tablespoon mineral powder
2 oz. water

Combine in your blender with:

1 teaspoon kelp
5 green olives, pitted
½ bunch mint leaves
2 oz. olive oil

Fave Bean Pesto

Steam for 10 minutes:

1 lb. fave beans
3 oz. water

Combine in your blender with:

2 cloves garlic, chopped
10 black olives, pitted
5 mushrooms
2 oz. olive oil

String bean pesto

Steam for 10 minutes:

1 lb. string beans

Combine in your blender with:

juice of 2 lemons
2 cloves garlic, chopped
½ lb. peas
1 teaspoon rosemary
2 oz. olive oil

These sauces are particularly good on spaghetti, grain dishes in general, baked eggplants, or sautéed zucchini.

Purées

A purée is a thickened sauce, usually made in a blender. I often serve purées on stuffed tomatoes, or over artichokes, or on top of baked potatoes. By themselves, purées make excellent snacks, thick and creamy.

AVOCADO PURÉE

Combine in your blender:

3 avocados
1 bunch chives, chopped
½ bunch garden cress, chopped
10 black olives, pitted
¼ red onion, coarsely chopped
1 tablespoon mineral powder
1 oz. olive oil
juice of 2 lemons (optional)

ASPARAGUS IN COLORS

Combine in your blender:

¼ lb. asparagus, coarsely chopped
¼ lb. mushrooms, steamed
¼ red onion, coarsely chopped
1 teaspoon kelp
1 teaspoon nutritional yeast
1 teaspoon mineral bouillon
¼ bunch parsley
liquid from steamed mushrooms
2 oz. olive oil
1½ oz. water

ORGANIC JOHN'S AVOCADO SPECIAL PURÉE

Combine in your blender:

3 avocados
1 tomato (hand-squeezed)
2 cloves garlic, chopped
1 bunch sweet basil
¼ bunch parsley
1 teaspoon mineral powder
1 teaspoon balanced protein seasoning
1 oz. olive oil

BEETS IN A RED GLOW

Combine in your blender:

6 small beets, cooked
1 small white onion, cooked
1 oz. mineral bouillon
juice of 1 lemon
¼ bunch garden cress
2 shallots, chopped
1 cucumber, peeled and cubed
2 oz. olive oil

BROCCOLI PURÉE

Combine in your blender:

1 bunch broccoli, chopped and briefly steamed
2 zucchini, chopped and briefly steamed
2 cloves garlic, chopped
1 teaspoon mineral powder
juice of 1 lemon
kernels from 2 ears uncooked corn
2 oz. olive oil

BRUSSELS SPROUTS PURÉE

Combine in your blender:

1 lb. Brussels sprouts, briefly steamed
1 large white onion, chopped and sautéed
1 tablespoon mineral powder
1 oz. mineral bouillon
1 clove garlic, chopped
½ oz. water
1 oz. olive oil

CARROT PURÉE

Combine in your blender:

6 carrots, briefly steamed
1 small sweet potato, sliced and sautéed
1 oz. mineral bouillon
¼ bunch parsley, chopped
2 stalks celery, chopped
juice from the cooked carrots
1 oz. olive oil

CAULIFLOWER PURÉE

Combine in your blender:

1 head cauliflower, chopped and briefly steamed
½ bunch broccoli, chopped and briefly steamed
¼ lb. peas
juice of 1 lemon
2 green onions, chopped
1 clove garlic, chopped
2 oz. olive oil

GREENS PURÉE

Combine in your blender:

½ bunch spinach, briefly steamed
½ bunch chicory, briefly steamed
½ bunch escarole, briefly steamed
2 cloves garlic, chopped
1 teaspoon kelp
1 teaspoon mineral powder
juice of 2 lemons
2 oz. olive oil

CUCUMBER PURÉE

Combine in your blender:

3 cucumbers, peeled and cubed
1 Belgian endive, chopped
1 tomato (hand-squeezed)
1 oz. mineral bouillon
1 teaspoon mineral powder
¼ bunch parsley
1 stalk celery, coarsely chopped
2 oz. olive oil

MUSHROOM PURÉE

½ lb. mushrooms
2 cloves garlic, chopped
2 oz. mineral bouillon
1 bunch garden cress
¼ bunch parsley
2 oz. olive oil

ONION PURÉE

Combine in your blender:

3 red onions, chopped and sautéed
1 bunch parsley
1 oz. mineral bouillon
1 tablespoon mineral powder
⅛ bulb anise
2 oz. olive oil

EGGPLANT AND GARBANZO BEAN PURÉE

Combine in your blender:

1 bunch parsley
10 black olives, pitted
2 cloves garlic, chopped
8 oz. garbanzo beans (soaked for 2 days, cooked for 25 minutes)
1 eggplant (baked in tinfoil, then cubed)
1 oz. mineral bouillon
4 oz. olive oil

PEA PURÉE

Combine in your blender:

2 lbs. peas
2 cloves garlic, chopped
¼ bunch spinach, briefly sautéed
1 red peper, chopped
1 teaspoon kelp
2 oz. olive oil

RED/GREEN PEPPER PURÉE

Combine in your blender:

3 red peppers, chopped and sautéed
2 green peppers, chopped and sautéed
1 potato, chopped and sautéed
10 black olives, pitted
1 clove garlic, chopped
1 oz. mineral bouillon
1 oz. olive oil

TURNIP PURÉE

Combine in your blender:

3 turnips, baked in tinfoil, then quartered
1 bunch spinach, briefly steamed
1 bunch parsley, chopped
juice of the steamed spinach
1 tablespoon mineral powder
½ white onion, chopped
2 oz. olive oil

EGGPLANT PURÉE

Combine in your blender:

1 eggplant, peeled and diced
crumbs from 2 slices homemade bread
¼ lb. mushrooms
2 oz. mineral bouillon
¼ bunch parsley, chopped
¼ bunch garden cress, chopped
2 shallots, chopped
2 oz. olive oil

Miso, a soya bean paste, can be used plain or as the base for these tasty miso purées which are especially delicious on vegetables. Preparation for each miso recipe is simple; just combine the ingredients in your blender.

MISO I

2 tablespoons miso
2 stalks celery, with leaves, chopped
5 black olives, pitted and chopped
2 cloves garlic, chopped
¼ bunch parsley, chopped
2 thin slices ginger root (optional)
2 oz. olive oil

MISO II

Add the juice of 2 lemons to the above recipe.

MISO III

Instead of juice, add ¼ lb. sautéed mushrooms.

MISO IV

Add lemon juice and sautéed mushrooms to the original recipe, plus 1 teaspoon sesame tahini.

MISO V

Add lemon juice, sautéed mushrooms, 1 teaspoon sesame tahini, and ½ bunch chopped steamed spinach.

Spreads

As the name implies, spreads are thick enough to spread—on bread, over salads, with vegetables. My favorites are the nut butters. Because of their nutritional qualities, nut butter spreads are an essential part of the universal menu. Best uncooked (they're higher in proteins and minerals when raw) nut butters add a creamy flavor and a delightful sensation to food. Common nut butters are made from almonds, cashews, sesame tahini, Brazil nuts, or peanuts. Popular combinations include almond cashew and cashew peanut spreads. You can make your own nut butters, from any nuts, if you have a powerful juicer. I've found the Champion juicer to be particularly good for this. You can also purchase nut butters at natural food stores.

Here are some nut butter possibilities to get you started: try any nut butter in a green salad; almond and cashew butter added to chopped steamed spinach; peanut butter added to baked zucchini; cashew butter with chopped cooked greens; sesame tahini with chopped baked eggplant, spinach, and tomato sauce; or Brazil nut butter added to baked squash. Nut butters provide a wonderful opportunity to experiment.

An unusual spread—no, not a nut butter—is an onion butter. I prepare it in fairly large quantities; keep it refrigerated.

ONION BUTTER

Peel and quarter 5 lbs. yellow onions. Place them in a heavy pot and cover with water. Bring contents to a full boil, cover pot, and then gently simmer for 24 hours. Add water as needed. When the onion residue has been simmered down to about 2½ pints of dark brown lumps, mash to a uniform consistency. Season to taste with kelp or mineral bouillon, and continue to simmer until excess liquid has evaporated. Bottle, refrigerate, and look forward to your next opportunity to use this delicious spread on whole grain breads, as a dip for raw vegetables, or as a garnish for cooked vegetables.

Chapter Ten

Grains, Greens, and Soya Beans

Grains

Grains are found in abundance in Nature's Garden. Each has its own special flavor and texture and, when eaten with salads or cooked vegetables, adds another nutritional dimension to our diet. Because they are bulky and because it is all too easy to get hooked on starches, I prefer to savor grains in small amounts.

I have had little experience either with oats or rye beyond knowing that the former is often used in cereals and cookies and the latter in breads. My preferences are for millet, buckwheat, barley, rice, and of course corn, a delightful and colorful companion in so many recipes. The beauty and flavor of corn should not be dimmed by cooking. Add it raw to salads or to already cooked foods.

When cooking grains, always add a tablespoon or so of mineral powder to the cooking water. Most grains should be boiled in a covered pan for twenty minutes and then cooked uncovered over a low flame for an additional ten minutes.

Whole wheat, the grain highest in protein and gluten, is especially delicious in homemade breads and cookies. However, the human body finds it difficult to digest wheat; additionally, many people are allergic to wheat. Use wheat and wheat products sparingly.

CREPES

Gather together these ingredients:

5 cups whole wheat pastry flour
1 tablespoon honey (optional)
water

Preheat a griddle at 450° for 10 minutes. Prepare a batter of 4 cups warm water, 5 cups whole wheat pastry flour, and honey, if desired. Reduce griddle to 350°. Pour a little oil on the griddle and wipe off immediately with a paper towel. Using a ladle, pour the mixed batter onto the griddle, spreading as you pour. Cook on one side, flip crepe, and continue cooking to desired texture and degree of doneness. Place on a flat serving platter; keep crepes warm until ready to use. They're excellent in Crepes alla Organic John.

Water and flour proportions can be varied, depending on the thickness of crepe you desire. This recipe should make enough for 4 to 6 persons.

CREPES ALLA ORGANIC JOHN

Gather together these ingredients:

4 to 6 crepes (see crepe recipe)
3 tomatoes
¼ lb. mushrooms, sliced
3 cloves garlic, minced
¼ bunch parsley, chopped
2 tablespoons sesame tahini
juice of 2 lemons
1 oz. mineral bouillon
½ red onion, finely sliced
1 lb. asparagus, chopped
2 leeks, diced
2 bunches spinach
olive oil
water

Sauté together for 8 minutes the mushrooms, tomatoes (hand-squeezed), garlic, and parsley. Add sesame tahini, mineral bouillon, and lemon juice; continue to cook for 5 more minutes. In another pan, sauté the onion, asparagus, and leeks in 2 oz. olive oil and 2 oz. water for about 5 minutes. In yet another pan, steam the spinach in 2 oz. water for 3 minutes. Do not chop the spinach. Lay the crepes flat; fill with the asparagus-leek mix and 1 tablespoon of the savory tomato sauce. Roll up each crepe, place it on a bed of spinach, and spoon the rest of the tomato sauce over all. Serve.

WHEAT DISCS

Gather together these ingredients:

½ lb. whole wheat pastry flour
1 to 2 tablespoons honey (optional)
4 to 6 cups water
olive oil

Mix flour, honey, and water together with an eggbeater. The amount of water you use depends on the thickness of batter desired. I prefer extremely thin wheat discs so I use a lot of water. Heat a grill at 450° for 10 minutes. Put olive oil on the grill and wipe off with a paper towel, leaving a thin coating. Reduce grill to 350°;

ladle batter onto grill into patties. Cook for 8 to 10 minutes, browning each side. This should make about 5 patties. Serve.

Millet, an alkaline grain, is high in protein. Delicate, light, and delicious, it is especially fine in this tasty vegetable dish.

MILLET WITH LIGHTLY COOKED VEGETABLES

Gather together these ingredients:

8 oz. millet
2 tablespoons mineral powder
½ cube soya butter
2 oz. mineral bouillon
¼ lb. mushrooms, sliced
1 cucumber, diced
2 Belgian endives, chopped
1 lb. peas
4 zucchini, chopped
1 bunch spinach
olive oil
water

Boil together 2 cups water and the mineral powder. Gently add millet to boiling water and lower the flame. Cook for 20 minutes covered; remove cover, and cook another 10 minutes over a very low flame. Then add soya butter and 1 oz. mineral bouillon. Recover pot and set aside.

Sauté together mushrooms, cucumber, endives, peas, and zucchini with 1 oz. mineral bouillon, 2½ oz. olive oil, and 2 oz. water. This should take about 5 to 8 minutes; while it's cooking you can steam the spinach in 2 oz. water for 3 minutes. Chop cooked spinach into small pieces and add to sautéed vegetables. Mix vegetables with millet, and serve.

My dog Rubio has a serving of millet with granulated almonds and seeds, steamed and raw vegetables, tofu, blended vitamin and mineral supplements, yeast, kelp, and the yolk of a raw egg four times a week. Millet is excellent for your pets.

Buckwheat, an alkaline grain, is quite high in vitamin E. As it produces heat quickly in the body, it's an excellent food for cold weather. Buckwheat spaghetti is one of my favorite wintertime concoctions. Prepare the sauce first, and then cook the noodles. Yeast is tasty sprinkled on top.

BUCKWHEAT SPAGHETTI NOODLES IN AN EGGPLANT-TOMATO SAUCE

Gather together these ingredients:

1 lb. buckwheat noodles
1 eggplant, peeled and diced
½ lb. asparagus, chopped
4 cloves garlic, minced
4 shallots, minced
½ red onion, finely sliced
1 oz. mineral bouillon
2 stalks celery, chopped
3 tomatoes
½ bunch sweet basil, chopped
10 black olives, pitted and minced
½ cube soya butter
olive oil
water

Sauté in a covered skillet for 5 minutes the garlic, shallots, onion, celery, and mineral bouillon in 2 oz. olive oil. Then add the tomatoes (hand-squeezed) and cook another 10 minutes. Add eggplant and asparagus and continue to cook for 10 to 15 minutes, removing the cover for the last 8 minutes. Mix in basil, olives, and 1 oz. olive oil. Set sauce aside while you prepare the noodles.

Add noodles and a little olive oil (to prevent sticking) to about 5 cups of boiling water. Cook for 5 to 10 minutes, drain, place on flat serving platter, and cover with eggplant-tomato sauce. Serve.

Barley is one of my favorite grains. It's easy to cook, easy to digest, and easy to eat.

BARLEY AND ME

Gather together these ingredients:

8 oz. barley
1 tablespoon mineral powder
1 teaspoon kelp
½ cube soya butter
½ bunch garden cress, finely chopped
¼ bunch parsley
3 green onions, chopped
1 bunch spinach
1 bunch escarole
1 oz. mineral bouillon
¼ lb. mushrooms, chopped
1 avocado, sliced
olive oil
water

Boil together 2 cups water, mineral powder, and kelp. Gently add barley to boiling water and lower the flame. Cook for 20 minutes covered; remove cover, and cook another 10 minutes over a very low flame. Then add soya butter, garden cress, parsley, and green onions. Stir well, recover pot, and set aside.

Sauté in a wok the spinach and escarole with mineral bouillon, 1 oz. olive oil, and 2 oz. water. After cooking 3 to 5 minutes, add this to the barley. Mix in chopped mushrooms and sliced avocado; serve.

Whole grain *brown rice* is highest in the B-complex vitamins; like barley it is easy to digest.

RICE-STUFFED TOMATOES

Gather together these ingredients:

2 cups rice, cooked
2 green onions, chopped
3 chives, chopped
1 oz. mineral bouillon
1 teaspoon kelp
½ bunch parsley, minced
1 cube soya butter
½ lb. mushrooms, chopped
1 bunch mustard greens, chopped
1 lb. pole beans, diced
6 large tomatoes
1 teaspoon mineral powder
olive oil
water

Prepare the rice your favorite way; I usually cook mine in a pressure cooker. Mix cooked rice with onions, chives, kelp, mineral bouillon, parsley, and ½ cube soya butter. Set aside while you sauté mushrooms and beans in 1 oz. olive oil and ½ oz. water. After about 8 minutes, add mustard greens and cook for another 5 minutes.

Meanwhile, hollow out tomatoes. Mix sautéed vegetables with rice and stuff this mixture into tomatoes. Place tomatoes in a deep skillet with ½ cube soya butter, mineral powder, and 2 oz. water. Cover and cook for 5 minutes; then serve.

Greens

The nutritional role of greens is vital to the Salade concept. Greens provide high quality, though limited, protein, and are brimming with vitamins and minerals, especially iron, folic acid, riboflavin, and calcium. They provide chlorophyll, which in turn furnishes the body with magnesium, so necessary for building healthy blood. The chlorophyll in the greens also supplies oxygen to the blood cells for the production of digestive bacteria.

I prefer my greens chopped fine in a raw or raw/cooked salad. Carefully wash greens to remove grit, and cut away any blemishes or tough stems. Cooked greens are best steamed in a stock of 3 oz. water with a little mineral bouillon. Generally steam greens no more than three minutes; the tougher greens—kale, mustard greens, and collard greens—may require five minutes. The stock of cooked greens is abundant in nutrient juices and makes an excellent drink. When cooking other vegetables add greens last, so they will not be overcooked.

The most readily available greens in the astonishing variety of Nature's Garden are:

beet tops
borage
catnip
chard
chervil
chicory
chives
collard greens
dandelion greens
endives
garden cress
kale
lettuce
mustard greens
parsley
sorrel
spinach
watercress

Soya Beans

Of all the foods in Nature's Garden, perhaps the most nutritional and versatile is the soya bean. Over 4,000 years ago the Chinese knew of its virtures and integrated the soya bean into their diet. Today, the Western world is becoming aware of the soya bean's high protein content and relatively low cost, and production continues to rise.

Nutritionists advocate widespread use of the soya bean and its derivatives as a partial answer to the world's food problems. It is readily cultivated and requires less commercial fertilizers than many other plant products. All eaters can profit from the substantial nutritional value of this cheap protein source.

Recent studies indicate:

1) Soya beans contain one and one-half times as much protein as cheese, peas, or lima beans; twice as much protein as meat or fish; three times as much protein as eggs or whole wheat flour, and eleven times as much protein as milk.

2) Soya beans contain fat-soluble lecithin, and are rich in phosphorus and choline. Lecithin extracted from soya beans is widely used in the commercial manufacture of bread, shortening, candy, and ice cream.

3) Soya beans contain half the amount of carbohydrates compared with all other beans.

4) Soya beans are rich in minerals and vitamins and certain alkaline salts.

The versatility of the soya bean can add new taste and nutritional dimensions to all menu planning whether in tofu, spreads, loaf dishes, sauces, or seasonings.

Japanese tofu (in Chinese, dou fu) is a bland, custard-like soya bean curd which absorbs the flavors of the foods cooked with it. Commercial tofu is available in produce or refrigerated sections of supermarkets and in Oriental food stores. It comes in varying degrees of firmness, from fresh and soft, to dense, dry-packed cubes. I prefer the fresh variety. Place it in a colander and gently turn for about five minutes, or squeeze until all the water has been drained.

For those who wish to make their own tofu, try the following recipe.

SOYA BEAN CURD (TOFU)

Gather together these ingredients:

2 cups dried soya beans, washed
1 teaspoon Epsom salts (optional)
water

Put soya beans in a large pot and cover with cold water. Soak overnight. Next morning, rinse the beans well, put them in your blender, and liquefy until very smooth, adding water as you go. The best way to do this is to put a small portion of beans in the blender; add water and blend, add more water if necessary, and then empty this portion into a bowl, and continue blending with another small portion. You'll probably use about 1 quart water for every cup of soaked beans.

Put liquefied beans in a clean dish towel or flour sack and squeeze out soya milk into a pan. Boil soya milk for 3 minutes. To hasten curdling, dissolve 1 teaspoon Epsom salts in ¼ cup warm water and slowly add to the milk, stirring all the while. After 5 to 10 minutes the milk will curdle. Gently lift the curd onto a dish towel or cheesecloth. Rinse carefully under gently running water, applying a little pressure to shape the curd. Set curd aside to drain—you can leave it in the dish towel, tie the dish towel ends together, and hang the tofu in the towel over the sink faucet. It should drain 2 to 3 hours. Put drained curd in a container, fill with cold water, cover, and refrigerate.

One pound of dry beans (about 2½ cups) yields about 2 pounds of curds.

Things you can do with tofu:

1. Add tofu to any of the vegetable complementary courses or companion dishes.
2. Cube and add to any or all green salads.
3. Sauté well-drained tofu with olive oil, or with cooked vegetables, or tomato sauce, or peppers and onions (a tasty companion dish), or choose your own favorite companion for this versatile food.
4. Sauté tofu in 1 teaspoon miso, 1 oz. mineral bouillon, and 2 oz. olive oil for about 3 minutes. You can use cubed tofu, or better yet, sauté 4 thick slices in this stock, turning each slice. The tofu slices can be mixed with vegetables, or topped with slices of tomato, avocado, or baked eggplant. Or serve the tofu on a thin crepe, topped with a vegetable purée. Or wrap tofu with spinach leaves or any green you like, cooked or raw. Or top tofu with whole or thickly sliced mushrooms. Or . . . well, it's up to you. Let your imagination take you on a tofu journey.

5. Make a tofu mix: take half of your homemade curd and mash with 1 avocado, 1 teaspoon mineral powder, 1 teaspoon balanced protein seasoning, ½ teaspoon kelp, ½ bunch chopped chives, 1 teaspoon olive oil, and 1 teaspoon mineral bouillon. This is a terrific stuffing for cooked tomatoes, squash, or eggplant. With the addition of slightly steamed peas, it is my favorite way to use tofu.

SOYA PATTIES

Gather together these ingredients:

1 lb. dry soya beans, washed
½ bunch chives, chopped
3 green onions, chopped
¼ bunch parsley, minced
¼ lb. black olives
2 red bell peppers, chopped
1 red onion, diced
½ lb. mushrooms, sliced
½ cube soya butter
olive oil
water

Put soya beans in a large cooking pot and cover with water. Soak overnight (or at least 12 hours). After soaking, cook beans in this water for 20 to 30 minutes. Drain well, and chop so beans are coarse and crunchy. Mix in chives, green onions, parsley, and black olives.

Set bean mixture aside while you sauté peppers, red onion, and mushrooms in 1 oz. olive oil and 1 oz. water for 5 minutes in an open skillet. When peppers are cooked, add soya butter, let melt, and mix well. Combine pepper mixture with soya beans. Make patties from this mixture and heat for 3 minutes on each side in an open skillet. Serve.

SOYA BEAN LOAF

Gather together these ingredients:

1 lb. dry soya beans, washed
½ lb. walnuts, chopped
2 slices homemade bread, made into crumbs
6 zucchini, diced
¼ lb. mushrooms, chopped
½ lb. asparagus, chopped
¼ cube soya butter
1 tablespoon mineral powder
kernels from 3 ears uncooked corn
olive oil
water

Put soya beans in a large cooking pot and cover with water. Soak overnight (or at least 12 hours). After soaking, cook beans in this water for 20 to 30 minutes. Drain well, and chop so beans are coarse and crunchy. Add walnuts and bread crumbs and mix well. Set bean mixture aside.

Preheat oven at 450° for 10 minutes. Sauté zucchini, mushrooms, and asparagus in soya butter, 2 oz. olive oil, and 1 oz. water. Cook them for 5 to 7 minutes in an open skillet, then add mineral powder. Mix together sautéed vegetables with soya bean-nut mixture. Form into a loaf and put into a baking pan. Reduce oven to 350° and bake for 7 to 10 minutes. Remove loaf from oven, top with corn kernels, and serve.

This is particularly appropriate as a complementing course.

GREEN SOYA BEAN MIX

Gather together these ingredients:

1 lb. dry green soya beans, washed
½ bunch chives
½ bunch sweet basil
1 tomato, quartered
½ avocado
3 carrots, finely diced
1 lb. peas
½ head romaine lettuce, chopped
olive oil
water

Put soya beans in a large cooking pot and cover with water. Soak for 2 days. Drain, and blend in your blender with chives, sweet basil, tomato, avocado, and 2 oz. olive oil. Place bean mix in a flat serving dish and surround with carrots, peas, and lettuce. Serve.

This is best served at room temperature as a companion dish.

SOYA BEANS IN A BEET STEW

Gather together these ingredients:

1 lb. dry soya beans, washed
1 red onion, thinly sliced
2 cloves garlic, minced
3 stalks celery, chopped
2 green bell peppers, chopped
10 small beets, quartered
kernels fom 3 ears uncooked corn
1 cube soya butter
4 oz. soya milk
2 tablespoons mineral powder
water

Put soya beans in a large cooking pot and cover with water. Soak overnight (or at least 12 hours). After soaking, cook beans in this water for 20 to 30 minutes. Drain well, and set aside.

Combine soya butter, red onion, garlic, celery, green peppers, beets, mineral powder, soya milk, and 8 oz. water. Cook over a low flame for 10 to 15 minutes. Add soya beans and cook for another 3 to 5 minutes. Put in a serving bowl and top with corn kernels. Serve.

You can vary the amount of water in the stock to produce the consistency you'd prefer. I like a stock that's nice and thick.

SOYA BEAN SPREAD

Gather together these ingredients:

1 lb. dry soya beans, washed
2 zucchini, diced
¼ lb. mushrooms, minced
3 stalks celery, diced
kernels from 2 ears uncooked corn
2 cloves garlic, minced
⅛ bunch parsley, chopped
⅛ bunch chives, chopped
2 oz. mineral bouillon
olive oil

Put soya beans in a large cooking pot and cover with water. Soak for 24 hours. Drain well, and mix in blender. Put blended soya beans in a round serving bowl. Mix in zucchini, mushrooms, celery, corn, garlic, parsley, chives, mineral bouillon, and 2 oz. olive oil. Mash into a creamy spread.

IMPROVISATIONS: If you wish, before draining beans, you may cook briefly—about 10 minutes. This spread is particularly good at lunchtime on thin slices of homemade bread or on thin homemade crepes.

Chapter Eleven

Fruit Delicacies

On Fruits

One's senses rejoice in the succulence and beauty of the fruits. What the great artists of the world have tried to capture on canvas, the eye can behold—the deep purples and reds of grapes and apples; the delicate hues of orange and yellow in tangerines, kumquats, mangos, bananas, and grapefruits; the regal splendor of the guava, tamarind, carob, and the entire melon family. The rare perfumes of sun-ripened fruits are sensual joys, and the sublime tastes of the various fruits are indescribable. Add to this zestful array—the look, smell, and taste of fruits—the knowledge that fruits contain the highest quality minerals and vitamins. . . . Ah, fruits are a nutritional nirvana.

Fruit Juices

Fruit juices are best in the morning, diluted with a little water. They should be taken sparingly, and like fruit, as a meal, not as a beverage with other foods. Besides enjoying such delights as plain fresh orange juice or grape juice, try some of these combinations. Use your juicer or blender to prepare.

ALMOND ORANGE JUICE

Blend together:

¼ lb. granulated almonds
8 oz. orange juice

PINEAPPLE ORANGE JUICE

Blend together:

1 pineapple, peeled and cut in chunks
6 oranges, peeled
1 tablespoon soyamel

PINEAPPLE STRAWBERRY JUICE

Blend together:

1 pineapple, peeled and cut in chunks
¼ lb. strawberries
1 teaspoon soyamel
1 teaspoon lecithin granules

COCONUT PAPAYA JUICE

Blend together:

milk from 2 coconuts
juice from 2 papayas

GUAVA NECTARINE JUICE

Blend together:

juice from 6 guavas
juice from 4 nectarines
1 teaspoon lecithin granules
¼ lb. granulated almonds

GRAPE BERRY JUICE

Blend together:

½ lb. grapes, seedless
¼ lb. berries (blueberries or huckleberries are best; don't use strawberries)
1 teaspoon lecithin granules
1 teaspoon vanilla

Fruit Salads

These simple and basic fruit salads will each serve about 4 to 6 persons. Prepare immediately before eating; peeled fruit, when allowed to sit too long, begins to lose its bright and pleasing appearance and its bountiful nutritional energies.

FRUIT QUICKIE

Place in a large bowl:

4 oranges, peeled and sliced
2 grapefruits, peeled and sliced
½ pineapple, peeled and diced

Toss in a handful of grated coconut and enjoy.

BANANA CREAM

Peel and slice:
5 bananas

Chop:
9 dates
1½ persimmons

Set aside. Combine in your blender:

1 banana
1 date
½ persimmon
1 teaspoon lecithin granules

Put chopped bananas in a bowl, top with chopped dates and persimmons, and pour blended mix over all.

CHERRY DELIGHT

Mix together:

1 lb. cherries, pitted and halved
4 peaches, quartered
3 nectarines, quartered

Top with 1 teaspoon soyamel.

SWEET DELIGHT

Mix together:

2 breadfruit innards
4 bananas, sliced
10 prunes, chopped
2 teaspoons lecithin granules

BERRIES TO CATCH THE EYE

Mix together:

1 lb. blueberries
¼ lb. raspberries
¼ lb. huckleberries

Berries can be topped with an avocado blend, or flavored with raw milk cottage cheese, or covered with a vanilla-soya milk-lecithin cream (see Apples on Top, below).

PROTEIN PLUS FRUIT SALAD

Mix together:

1 head bibb lettuce, chopped
3 oranges, peeled and chopped
3 apples, chopped
½ pineapple, peeled and chopped
3 stalks celery, chopped
6 oz. cottage cheese

In place of the cottage cheese, you could add 6 oz. chopped nuts, or 1 chopped avocado; if using nuts or avocado, add 1 tablespoon lecithin granules and 1 teaspoon soyamel.

APPLES ON TOP

Thinly slice:

15 dates, pitted
2 pears
5 apples

Place in bowl with apples on top and cover with a vanilla cream: 2 teaspoons vanilla, 4 oz. soya milk, and 1 teaspoon lecithin granules mixed together.

MULTICOLOR FRUIT SALAD

Blend together:

2 tablespoons pineapple
1 teaspoon red currants
1 avocado

Pour over:

1 pineapple, peeled and chopped
4 oranges, peeled and chopped
¼ lb. red currants

MELON DELIGHT

Mix together melon balls from:

½ Persian melon
½ cantaloupe
½ watermelon

TROPICAL DELIGHT

Mix together:

4 mangos, peeled and diced
3 guavas, mashed
2 persimmons, diced

Stuff into 2 large papayas, halved and seeded, and top with the gratings of ½ coconut.

APRICOTS AND PLUMS

Mix together:

12 apricots, halved and pitted
12 plums, halved and pitted

In your blender make a thick cream of ½ lb. pitted cherries, and 2 bananas. Pour over the apricots and plums.

CREPE SUPREME

Combine in your blender:

4 bananas
4 figs
2 breadfruit innards

Stuff mixture in the center of an especially thin crepe (see section on grains). Top with melted carob.

ALMOND PIE

Granulate 1 lb. almonds in your nutgrinder (or blender). Spread about a third of them on the bottom of a serving bowl.

Slice:

1 pineapple, peeled (8 thin slices)
3 oranges, peeled (5 thin slices each)
¼ lb. strawberries (3 slices each)

Alternate layers of almonds and fruit in bowl, ending with pineapple.

AVOCADOS AND FRUITS

Cover bottom of a serving bowl with:

2 big avocados, mashed

Cover avocado with:

¼ lb. strawberries, mashed
¼ lb. blueberries, mashed

Cover berries with:

1 pineapple, peeled and chopped
2 oranges, peeled and chopped
1 mango, chopped

STUFFED APPLES

Dig out the centers, about three-quarters of the way down, of:

6 apples

Mix together:

the cut-out part of the apple (minus the seeds and core membranes)
3 mangos, diced
3 peaches, diced
1 persimmon, diced

Fill the apples with the stuffing.

Fruit Sherbets

These sherbets come deliciously alive with the aid of a juicer, an essential tool for every kitchen where nutritional foods are appreciated. I feel the Champion and Acme juicers rank supreme in the preparation of juices, nut butters, and sherbets. All the juices used in these sherbets recipes are to be made immediately before sherbet preparation. The use of natural vanilla, carob, and lecithin granules to produce a creamy texture, and soyamel, a powder made from soya beans, is suggested. I do not recommend the use of artificial sweeteners, artificial colors, or honey. So with a bag of mixed fruit, a juicer, and a blender we enter Sherbet World.

Sherbet making is a simple process. These basic instructions will allow you to make exquisite treats from the ingredients that follow.

1) Prepare juices in your juicer.
2) Combine juices and all other ingredients in blender.
3) Pour blended mixture into freezing trays and freeze until solid.
4) When mixture is frozen, cut it in strips thin enough to fit into the throat of your juicer.
5) Assemble the juicer for homogenizing and homogenize the frozen strips.
6) Serve instantly.

If the mixture is too thick, reduce or omit the lecithin granules. These recipes will make one to one-half quarts sherbet. All fruits are, as appropriate, pitted, cored, or peeled.

APPLE AND APRICOT SHERBET

1½ cups apricot juice
1½ cups apple juice
3 apricots, chopped
2 apples, peeled and chopped
2 tablespoons lecithin granules
2 tablespoons soyamel
1 teaspoon vanilla

MELON SHERBET

(Use any variety of melons)

2 cups mixed watermelon and cantaloupe juice
¼ cantaloupe
¼ watermelon
3 tablespoons lecithin granules
2 tablespoons soyamel
1 teaspoon vanilla

BANANA-DATE-FIG SHERBET

3 cups fig juice
2 bananas
6 dates
2 tablespoons soyamel
1 teaspoon carob

GRAPE AND BERRY SHERBET

(Use any variety of berries)

3 cups mixed grape and berry juice
¼ lb. seedless grapes and berries mixed
juice of 1 lemon
2 tablespoons lecithin granules
3 tablespoons soyamel
1 teaspoon vanilla

ORANGE AND PINEAPPLE SHERBET

3 cups mixed orange and pineapple juice
½ pineapple, diced
2 oranges, diced
2 tablespoons lecithin granules
2 tablespoons soyamel
1 teaspoon vanilla

LEMON-LIME-TANGERINE SHERBET

3 cups mixed lemon, lime, and tangerine juice
2 tablespoons lecithin granules
2 tablespoons soyamel
1 teaspoon vanilla

PEACH AND PERSIMMON SHERBET

- 2 cups mixed peach and persimmon juice
- 2 peaches, chopped
- 1 persimmon, chopped
- 2 tablespoons lecithin
- 2 tablespoons soyamel
- 1 teaspoon vanilla

MANGO-PAPAYA-AVOCADO SHERBET

- 3 cups mixed mango and papaya juice
- 1 mango, chopped
- ¼ papaya, chopped
- 1 avocado, chopped
- 2 tablespoons lecithin granules
- 2 tablespoons soyamel
- 1 teaspoon vanilla

GUAVA AND TAMARIND SHERBET

- 3 cups mixed guava and tamarind juice
- 2 guavas, chopped
- 1 tamarind, chopped
- 2 tablespoons lecithin granules
- 2 tablespoons soyamel
- 1 teaspoon vanilla

Fruit Creams

Now let's explore some unfrozen mixtures; these creams are prepared by following the first two steps in making fruit sherbets: make juices in your juicer; combine them and all other ingredients in your blender. These are *not* frozen.

THE ROSE

Spread gently the petals of four roses from your garden. Fill the centers with the mango-papaya-avocado sherbet mixture, blended to a cream.

ORANGE RIND

Halve and peel four oranges, leaving the skins whole, like little cups. Make a banana-date-fig sherbet; add the orange sections and cream well. Fill the orange rinds with this mixture.

COCONUT DELIGHT

Carefully saw a coconut in half. Use the coconut milk and meat to blend with the peach and persimmon sherbet until creamy.

SILLY PINEAPPLE

Slice a pineapple in half and carefully remove the flesh to leave a neatly webbed shell. Stuff with a grape and berry sherbet mixture blended until creamy smooth.

These creamy unfrozen mixtures can also make exquisite desserts when served in chilled glasses. They are fair combinations for the gourmet's palate, for infrequent indulgence with love and variety.

CHILLED ORANGE PINEAPPLE CREAM WITH CASHEW BUTTER

Line the bottom of chilled brandy snifter with creamy cashew butter. Cover the cashew butter with a layer of orange and pineapple sherbet mixture blended until creamy. Top with coconut shavings.

CHILLED PEACH AND PERSIMMON CREAM WITH ALMONDS

Line the bottom of a chilled cup with granulated almonds. Cover these with a peach and persimmon sherbet mixture blended until creamy. Top with chopped Brazil nuts and raisins.

CHILLED CITRUS CREAM WITH COCONUT

Line the bottom of a chilled brandy snifter with shaved coconut. Cover this with a lemon-lime-tangerine sherbet mixture blended until creamy smooth. Top with sliced cherries and red currants.

CHILLED APPLE-APRICOT CREAM WITH NUTS

Line the bottom of a chilled wine glass with granulated almonds, cashews, and coconut. Cover this with an apple and apricot sherbet mixture blended until creamy smooth. Top with granulated nuts and dried pineapple.

Chapter Twelve

The Fine Art of Eating (with Selected Menus)

For the most part, eating is a conditioned response—three times a day, hungry or not, we think we must eat. Each time, the most important factor is the clock, not nourishment.

The fine art of eating, once associated with the landed gentry and elegant surroundings, belongs to all of us. It is not damask tablecloths or heirloom silver; it *is* simply making our minds and bodies conscious of what should be eaten and how it should be prepared. Such a concept is hardly a discovery, but rather a rediscovery. Nature's Garden has been with us since long before the tyranny of the clock.

These menus are examples of meal planning. I've set forth suggestions for three meals a day, plus an occasional afternoon delicacy, with the main meal in the evening. Like it or not, this is the standard American eating pattern. However, eating only when hungry is the best plan, and then eat only enough to satisfy, not to stupefy.

Inquiry, flexibility, and creativity are your keys to unlock all the nutritional excitements found in Nature's Garden. The fine art of eating can then be yours to enjoy.

Selected Menus

BREAKFAST
Two glasses* of mixed vegetable juices—carrot, celery, apple, and beet—combined well with blended almonds

LUNCH
Small green salad, with eggplant purée on a slice of whole wheat toast

AFTERNOON DELICACY
Small fruit salad—mango, papaya, and apricots—with 4 oz. raw milk cottage cheese, granulated nuts, or nut butter.

DINNER
Large green salad
Complementing course: Asparagus in Crepes
Companion dish: Chopped Eggplant with Peas

* Throughout these menus, a glass means 8 liquid ounces. But be flexible; listen to your body.

BREAKFAST
Two glasses* of mixed vegetable juices—carrot, celery, spinach, and cabbage.

LUNCH
Raw cooked salad (try Sweet Potato and Greens)
Fresh broccoli purée with uncooked peas

DINNER
Large green salad
Complementing course: Broccoli and Red Peppers in Raw and Cooked Mushroom Sauce
Companion dish: Soya Patties

BREAKFAST
Glass of warm water with juice of 1 lemon
One glass of mixed vegetable juices—carrot, celery, cucumber, and lettuce

LUNCH
Small green salad with soya beans, fresh peas, and onion purée

DINNER
Large green salad
Complementing course: Soya Bean Loaf
Companion dish: Carrots Lightly

BREAKFAST
Glass of Almond Orange Juice
Grape Berry Sherbet

LUNCH
Fresh fruit salad with avocado cream dressing

* Throughout these menus, a glass means 8 liquid ounces. But be flexible; listen to your body.

DINNER
Large green salad with almond and cashew butter dressing
Complementing course: Cauliflower under Green
Companion dish: Broccoli and tomato

BREAKFAST
Two glasses of mixed vegetable juices—carrot, cucumber, parsley, and apple

LUNCH
Raw/cooked salad of Eggplant and Greens, with onion purée

AFTERNOON DELICACY
Soya patties with tomato, cucumber, and garden cress salad

DINNER
Large green salad
Complementing course: Spaghetti with Asparagus and Tomato Sauce
Companion dish: Beans and Peas in Red Peppers

BREAKFAST
Glass of warm water with juice of 1 lemon
One glass of mixed vegetable juices—carrot, apple, celery, cucumbers, and beet

LUNCH
Melon Delight fruit salad
Melon Sherbet

AFTERNOON DELICACY
Avocado salad with sautéed green vegetables covered with onion and mushroom purée

DINNER
Green salad
Complementing course: Asparagus and Sweet Potatoes
Companion dish: Colorful Peppers

BREAKFAST
Fruit salad—pineapple, oranges, persimmons, and mangos—with 6 oz. raw milk cottage cheese, nuts, or nut butter

LUNCH
Crepe alla Organic John
Green salad

AFTERNOON DELICACY
A fruit cream or sherbet

DINNER
Large green salad with avocado dressing
Complementing course: Tomatoes Lightly
Companion dish: Eggplant Sunshine

This Is My Day

I want to share a day with you, so you can see how a love of Nature's Garden and an understanding of the precepts of Salade can flavor one's life.

Each day, I awake leisurely and naturally, then jog a few miles in an unhurried manner—just early enough to enjoy the serenity and beauty of Nature before most households sit down to their first cup of coffee. After returning home and showering, I prepare in my blender a quart of vegetable juice mixed with seeds, instant protein powder, almonds, and wheat germ. To best savor the juice's delightful flavors, I drink it neither hot nor cold, but perhaps closer to the temperature of Nature's Garden. Half of the juice I drink immediately and the other half I put in a bottle for later in the morning. I always have a blend of 1 tablespoon wheat germ oil and the yolk of a raw egg when the weather is damp and rainy; if sunny I take just the wheat germ oil.

If I am going to be away from the house for the day, I prepare a container of salad or of something cooked, plus a bag of fruit and some nut butter. And I always remember those sidewalk lunches in Brooklyn as I gather together my meal. Toward the end of the day I nourish my self with the serenity and company of good friends and the zest and flavor of good food. As day closes, I like to exchange a few thoughts with the plants that grace the house or the stars that illuminate the skylight. It has been a good day.

Chapter Thirteen

Exercise

When Russian physiologist Ivan Pavlov was asked why he spent so much time in his garden, he replied, "To give joy to my muscles."

Exercise and the proper diet combined permit the human body to function at maximum capacity while conditioning and preserving it. When all is in concert—diet, exercise, and philosophical outlook—the human being is the most exquisite ballet, capable of infinite tasks and inner satisfactions.

Exercise takes several different forms. There is the exercise of daily living (carrying groceries, for example), exercise resulting from one's occupation (driving a bus or loading a truck), and exercise commonly called recreational exercise, perhaps because we've been taught that it is non-essential and even frivolous. The types of exercises I will describe here will fall into this third category. I see this third type of exercise as any physical activity which trains or develops the body; it should involve systematic practice of bodily exertion for the sake of the body's health. Exercise is fun through which we can build a strong, healthy body in harmony with the mind.

Calisthenics are light exercises or gymnastics, including sit-ups, push-ups, and jumping jacks, with an emphasis on building the skeletal muscles. Calisthenics and memories of P.E. class are in the minds of many when they reject "exercise."

Dancing is a rhythmic, refreshing, and enjoyable way of expressing yourself to music. It builds mind-body coordination, promotes grace and poise, and tones muscles, joints, glands, and the respiratory and digestive organs.

Jogging, best defined as running slowly enough to carry on a conversation, improves your lungs, heart, and circulatory system by expanding their capacity to handle stress. It builds muscles tone, reduces hips and thighs, redistributes weight, and flattens the abdomen. I have experienced best results from not alternating walking and running, but rather keeping a steady pace—perhaps sprinting periodically, but never coming to a standstill and then starting again. Once I stop running, I walk the remaining distance at a slow and leisurely pace. This is my jogging style; try different methods until you find your own.

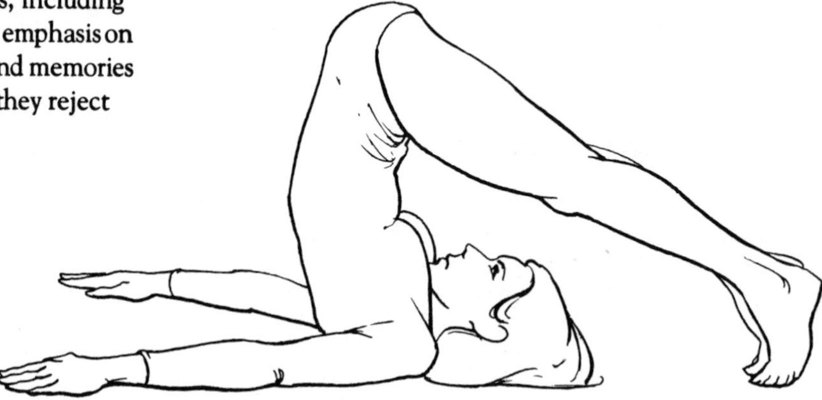

Yoga is the precise practice of stretching for maximum health. It is a most natural exercise directed at increasing the flow of blood to the tissues and cells, and increasing oxygenation. Mild stretching exercises are most beneficial upon awakening, before shower or breakfast. Yoga is not exercise as we of the West know it, but rather *asana*, or postures performed with utmost ease and comfort. Yoga concentrates on the body's nerve centers and the endocrine system. It builds and tones the subtle nerves of the spinal column. Yoga massages, stretches, and mellows.

Walking is one of the best overall exercises; it tunes the entire system. It increases the rate of metabolism, thus burning fat and promoting weight loss. Blood pressure, cholesterol, and sugar levels in the blood tend to fall. Heart muscles and lung capactiy develop.

Isotonic exercises involve progressive resistance and repetition to increase the strength of muscle groups. Weightlifting is the major isotonic exercise, and it's great for strengthening muscles and improving muscle tone. Traditionally associated with sweaty Olympic champions, weightlifting has lately gained a wider acceptance. It is useful for building skeletal muscles, but has little effect on the body's endurance or ability to handle stress.

Isometric exercises are somewhat similar to weightlifting in that skeletal muscles are toned and built by the tensing of muscles in opposition to another set of muscles or an immovable object. However, isometrics are motionless; therein lies the positive (easy to do on the bus in the morning) and the negative (no benefits to circulatory systems, no increase in the body's ability to deal with stress).

Sport-oriented exercises include such traditional activities as swimming, tennis, bicycling, racketball, golf, skating, horseback riding, and so on.

The need for exercise varies and in each person is determined by the weakest organ. This "weakest organ" test also applies to the limits you must put on exercise. If, for example, you have respiratory problems (weakest organ: lungs), a program of long effortless walks would be best, perhaps eventually extended into easy jogging. But if your jogging graduates into running, and your weakest organ is huffing and puffing, listen to your body. Respect the point of fatigue and the limits of your body. The American Association for Health, Physical Education, and Recreation offers these guidelines:

Refrain from exercise when breathing and heartbeat are still greatly elevated ten minutes after exercise; refrain from exercise when fatigue persists after a two-hour rest period; refrain from exercise if you experience restlessness and broken sleep or a sense of fatigue the day following strenuous exercise. In all of these cases, refrain and rest; if symptoms continue, consult a physician.

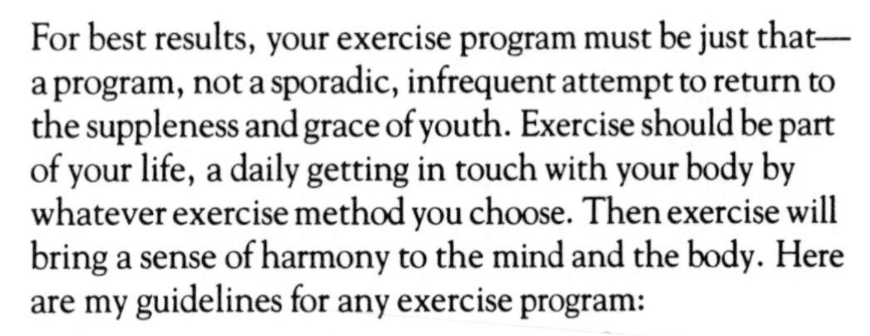

For best results, your exercise program must be just that—a program, not a sporadic, infrequent attempt to return to the suppleness and grace of youth. Exercise should be part of your life, a daily getting in touch with your body by whatever exercise method you choose. Then exercise will bring a sense of harmony to the mind and the body. Here are my guidelines for any exercise program:

1) Exercise should be regular and applied with concentration and discipline.
2) Exercise should be compatible with your needs. Being able to lift 150 pounds may be a useless skill to a secretary, but essential to a backpacker. Listen to your life's needs.
3) Exercise should not involve stress, strain, or competition.
4) Exercise should be simple, the costs minimal, the time needed flexible.
5) Exercise should reward regular practice with increased endurance and strength and joy.
6) Exercise must be exciting, fun, a challenge.

A Balanced Exercise Program Will:

1) Impart vigor and activates all organs.
2) Strengthen blood vessels, lungs, heart; improve transfer of oxygen to the cells and increase circulation of blood and lymph systems.
3) Stimulate processes of digestion, absorption, metabolism, and elimination.
4) Improve tone and quality of muscle tissues.
5) Develop symmetry of the body.
6) Help in corrective development (exercise as therapy).
7) Foster strong will and determination.
8) Build mind-body coordination.
9) Offer a poised, graceful body.
10) Enhance one's kinesthetic intelligence, or pleasure in movement.

Bibliography

Acharya, Pundit. *Studies in Neuro-Bio-Electronics.* Two volumes. Prana Press, 1970.

Aihara, Herman. *Acid and Alkaline.* George Ohsawa Macrobiotic Foundation, 1971.

Airola, Paavo. *Are You Confused?* Health Plus, 1974.

———. *Health Secrets from Europe.* Arc, 1971.

———. *How to Get Well.* Health Plus, 1974.

———. *How to Keep Slim, Healthy, and Young with Juice Fasting.* Health Plus, 1971.

Armstrong, J.W. *Water of Life.* True Health Publishing, 1944.

Bieler, Henry. *Food is Your Best Medicine.* Random House, 1965.

Bragg, Paul. *The Bragg System.* Health Science, 1964.

Brandt, Johanna. *Grape Cure.* Provoker Press, 1969.

C., B.H. *About Hypoglycemia.* Karpat Publishing, 1971.

———. *Low Blood Sugar.* Karpat Publishing, 1971.

Carqué, Otto. *Rational Diet.* Health Research, 1971.

———. *Vital Facts About Food.* Published by the author, 1974.

Carter, Richard. *Doctor's Business.* Doubleday, 1959.

Cheraskin, E.; William Ringsdorf; and J.W. Clark. *Diet and Disease.* Rodale Books, 1970.

Day, Harvey. *About Fluoridation.* Thorsons, 1966.

De Coti Marsh, Charles. *Prescription for Energy.* Thorsons, 1961.

Dubos, Rene. *Mirage of Health.* Harper & Row, 1959.

Ehret, Arnold. *Mental Dietetics.* Ehret Literature Publishing Co., 1971.

———. *Mucusless Diet Healing System.* Ehret Literature Publishing Co., 1971.

———. *Rational Fasting.* Ehret Literature Publishing Co., 1971.

———. *Thus Speaketh the Stomach.* Ehret Literature Publishing Co., 1971.

Esser, William. *Dictionary of Man's Food.* Natural Hygiene Press, 1972.

Fortune Magazine, Editors. *Our Ailing Medical System.* Harper & Row, 1969.

Fredericks, Carlton. *Food Facts and Fallacies.* Arco, 1965.

———. "Hypoglycemia." Nutritional Update, Spring 1974.

———. *Low Blood Sugar and You.* Grosset & Dunlap, 1969.

Gerson, Max. *Cancer Therapy.* Dura Books, 1958.

Graham, Sylvester; Russell Trall; and Herbert Shelton. *Natural Hygiene.* Natural Hygiene Press, 1972.

Graves, W.H. *Medicinal Value of Natural Foods.* Published by the author, 1971.

Hauser, Gayelord, and Ragmar Berg. *Dictionary of Food.* Benedict Lust Publications, 1970.

Hawken, Paul, and Fred Rohe. *The Oil Story.* Distributed by Organic Merchants, 1970.

———. *The Salt Story.* Distributed by Organic Merchants, 1970.

Heritage, Ford. *Composition and Facts About Foods.* Health Research, 1971.

Hinman, Robert, and Robert Harris. *Story of Meat.* Swift & Co., 1947.

Hughes, Albert. *About Allergy.* Thorsons, 1966.

Hunter, Beatrice. *Consumer Beware.* Simon & Schuster, 1971.

Jensen, Bernard. *Collected Pamphlets* (including *How to Enjoy Better Health from Natural Remedies; How to Relax and Relieve Tension; How to Revitalize the Glands; Health for Our Children; Special Foods for Special Needs;* and *Blood, the Essence of Life)*. Bernard Jensen Products Publishing Division, 1970.
Kahn, Fritz. *Man in Structure and Function.* Two volumes. Knopf, 1960.
Kelley, William. *New Hope for Cancer Victims.* Kelley Research Foundation, 1969.
Kirschner, H.E. *Live Food Juices.* H.C. White Publications, 1962.
———. *Nature's Seven Doctors.* H.C. White Publications, 1962.
Kriyananda. *Yoga Postures for Self-Realization and Awareness.* Onanda Publications, 1969.
Kulvinskas, Viktoras. *Love Your Body.* Hippocrates Health Institute, 1972.
Louise, Mira. *Acid-Alkaline Balance.* New Horizons, 1970.
Lust, Benedict. *Blood-Washing Method.* Published by the author, 1970.
———. *The Internal Uncleanliness of Man.* Published by the author, 1970.
Lust, John. *About Raw Juices.* Thorsons, 1972.
———. *Drink Your Troubles Away.* Benedict Lust Publications, 1967.
———. *Raw Juice Therapy.* Thorsons, 1969.
Norris, P.E. *About Fruits and Vegetables and Salads.* Thorsons, 1968.
———. *About Honey.* Thorsons, 1968.
———. *About Milk, Cheese, and Eggs.* Thorsons, 1968.
———. *About Nuts and Dried Fruits.* Thorsons, 1968.
———. *About Yeast.* Thorsons, 1968.
———. *About Yoghurt.* Thorsons, 1968.
Nutrition Search, Inc. *Nutrition Almanac.* McGraw-Hill, 1975.
Ohsawa, George. *Cancer and the Philosophy of the Far East.* Swan House, 1971.
Powell, W.A. Erick. *Building a Healthy Heart.* Health Sciences Press, 1970.
Rodale, J.I. *Natural Health, Sugar, and the Criminal Mind.* Pyramid Books, 1968.
Satchidananda, Swami. *Integral Yoga Postures—Hatha Yoga.* Holt, 1970.
Shelton, Herbert M. *Fasting Can Save Your Life.* Natural Hygiene Press, 1967.
———. *Food Combining Made Easy.* Dr. Shelton's Health School, 1951.
———. *The Hygienic System.* Five volumes. Dr. Shelton's Health School, 1963.
———. *Superior Nutrition.* Dr. Shelton's Health School, 1975.
Skinner, B.F. *About Behaviorism.* Knopf, 1974.
Slagle, Bob. *Sojourn in Nutritional Lane.* Published by the author, 1973.
Snyder, Arthur. *Nature's Way to Health.* Hansen's Publishers, 1970.
———. *Vitamins and Minerals.* Hansen's Publishers, 1970.
Stevenson, Scott. *Universal Home Doctor.* Prentice-Hall, 1965.
Stone, Randolph. *Polarity Therapy, and all Selected Writings.* Sharma as the Tribune Press, 1969.
———. *A Purifying Diet.* Published by the author, 1954.
Tilden, J.H. *Toxemia Explained.* Health Research, 1967.
Veith, Ilza. *Yellow Emperor's Classic of Internal Medicine.* University of California Press, 1973.
Walker, N.W. *Diet and Salad Suggestions.* Norwalk Press, 1970.
Weger, George. *Dietetic Disappointments and Failures.* Health Research, 1960.
Wigmore, Ann. *Health, the Organic Way.* Hippocrates Health Institute, 1960.
Wilkins, Juan Ammon. *Coconuts and Constipation.* Massa Press, 1934.
Wood, Curtis, Jr. *Overfed But Undernourished.* Exposition Press, 1959.
Yogananda, Paramansa. *Autobiography of a Yogi.* Self-Realization Fellowship, 1959.

Appendix I

The Garden's Nutrition: Vitamins, Minerals, Proteins

Vitamins and Minerals

The varied foods of Nature's Garden provide humankind with essential and mysterious nutritional substances: vitamins and minerals. Their actions and interactions within the body are still under intense scientific study. We do know that vitamins, complex organic substances found in miniscule quantities in many foods, act as catalysts in activating the chemical processes of the body. Minerals, also occurring in exceedingly small amounts in many foods, contribute to the building process within the body or to the functioning of one of the body's systems.

Specific deficiencies of a certain vitamin or mineral can be measured by a physician only as related to one's unique body chemistry. However, combinations of food as recommended by the Salade concept will provide adequate amounts of all the vitamins and minerals for most people. If you are interested in the exact quantities of vitamins and minerals in various foods, read the *Nutrition Almanac,* put together by Nutrition Search, Inc.

As children of the twentieth century we are intellectually aware of the importance of vitamins and minerals, yet still we feed on undergrown, overcooked semi-foods and wonder why we don't feel better. When I encounter someone who is complacent about the role of vitamins and minerals in good nutrition, I suggest they read the following list. It think it clearly indicates where Nature's life-giving vitamins and minerals can be found, how the body makes use of them, and how the body suffers from a lack of them.

I've also indicated the RDA, or Recommended Dietary Allowance,* as established by the Food and Nutrition Board of the National Research Council. RDA's are a nutritional standard of recommended intakes of nutrients for the maintenance of good health. This recommended allowance is usually higher then the MDR (Minimum Daily Adult Requirement, another standard sometimes seen); RDA'S indicate what an adult needs to maintain health, not just what he can scrape by with. During illness or stress, even this allowance may not be sufficient.

RDA's given here are for average-sized adult males living in a temperate climate, with average daily energy expenditure and stress. Larger tables of RDA's are available in many nutrition books and should be consulted to determine the exact vitamin and mineral requirements for females (especially during pregnancy and lactation), children, and infants. RDA's are given in the appropriate and generally accepted measure: micrograms, milligrams, or International Units.

I have included all major sources of vitamins and

* Not to be confused with the United States Recommended Daily Allowance (USRDA), which is derived from RDA but used more for nutritional labeling.

minerals, including many that are not in concert with the Salade concept: liver, for example. Please consider this a compilation of nutrient possibilities, and not necessarily recommendations from the Natural Chef.

Vitamins*

VITAMIN A (Retinol)

Sources: Liver, fish liver oils, carrots, tomatoes, pumpkin, broccoli, dark green leafy vegetables, dairy products, eggyolks only, mangoes, apricots, yellow melons, and peaches.

Functions: Builds resistance to infections, especially of the respiratory tract. Helps maintain healthy skin and organ tissues. Necessary in the formation of visual purple, which counteracts night blindness and weak eyesight. Essential for healthy pregnancy and lactation.

Deficiency: May result in retarded growth, decreased resistance to infection, dry and scaly skin, night blindness, loss of vigor, and defective teeth and gums.

RDA: 5,000 International Units.

VITAMIN B_1 (Thiamine)

Sources: Nutritional yeast, rice husks, whole grains, peanuts, most vegetables, and milk.

Functions: Aids growth and digestion; essential for normal functioning of nerve tissues, muscles, and heart.

Deficiency: May result in loss of appetite, weakness, nervous irritability, insomnia, loss of weight, vague aches and pains, mental depression, and constipation. May inhibit growth in children.

RDA: 1.4 mg. For best results, thiamine should be taken with all other vitamins of the B-complex.

VITAMIN B_2 (Riboflavin)

Sources: Almonds (best source), sunflower seeds, nutritional yeast, wheat germ, milk, cheese, whole grains, liver, and cooked leafy vegetables.

Functions: Essential for growth and general health. Promotes healthy eyes, skin, nails, and hair. May aid the prevention of cataracts.

Deficiency: May result in bloodshot eyes, abnormal sensitivity to light, itching and burning of eyes, inflammations of the mouth and tongue, cracks on lips and at corners of mouth, dull or oily hair and skin, premature wrinkles on face and arms, eczema, and split nails. Can be a partial cause of seborrhea, anemia, vaginal itching, cataracts, and ulcers.

RDA: 1.6 mg.

VITAMIN B_3 (Niacin)

Sources: Nutritional yeast, wheat germ, rice bran and polishings, nuts, sunflower seeds, whole grains, green vegetables, and liver.

Functions: Helps prevent pellagra. Essential to proper functioning of the circulatory and nervous systems and to proper protein and carbohydrate metabolism. Maintains normal functions of gastro-intestinal tract; promotes healthy skin. May prevent migraine headaches and schizophrenia.

Deficiency: May result in coated tongue, canker sores, irritability, nervousness, skin lesions, diarrhea, memory loss, headaches, insomnia, digestive disorders, and anemia.

RDA: 18 mg.

VITAMIN B_5 (Pantothenic Acid)

Sources: Nutritional yeast, wheat germ and bran, royal jelly, whole grains, green vegetables, peas, beans, peanuts, blackstrap molasses, liver, and egg yolks.

Functions: Important for all vital functions of the body, including production of adrenal hormones; aids normal development of the central nervous system; protects against physical and mental stresses, and against damage from radiation.

Deficiency: May result in chronic fatigue, decreased resistance to infections, graying and loss of hair, dizziness,

* Much of this information is adapted from material in Paavo Airola's *How to Get Well,* Ford Heritage's *Composition and Facts about Foods,* and *The Nutritional Almanac,* by Nutrition Search, Inc.

depression, irritability, muscular weakness, stomach distress, and constipation. May lead to skin disorders, retarded growth, inflammation of the feet, insomnia, muscle cramps, adrenal exhaustion, low blood sugar (hypoglycemia), low blood pressure, and possibly asthma and allergies.

RDA: Not yet established; many authorities recommend 30 to 50 mg. a day.

VITAMIN B_6 (Pyridoxine)

Sources: Nutritional yeast, bananas, avocados, wheat germ and bran, soya beans, walnuts, blackstrap molasses, cantaloupe, cabbage, egg yolks, liver, green leafy vegetables, green bell peppers, carrots, peanuts, and pecans. Cooking and processing foods destroys vitamin B_6.

Functions: Involved in protein and fatty acid metabolism and in the formation of antibodies which protect against bacterial invasions. Activates enzymes and enzyme systems, is essential to the structure and function of DNA and RNA, and aids nervous system and brain function. Important for normal reproductive processes. Helps prevent acne, tooth decay, diabetes, heart disease, epileptic seizures, and various nervous disorders. Can be effective as a natural diuretic. Required for the absorption of vitamin B_{12} and the production of hydrochloric acid.

Deficiency: May result in anemia, edema, depression, acne, sore mouth and lips, eczema, kidney stones, inflammation of the colon, insomnia, tooth decay, irritability, loss of muscular control, and migraine headaches.

RDA: 2.0 mg.

CHOLINE (A B-complex Vitamin)

Sources: Granular or liquid lecithin (from soya beans), nutritional yeast, wheat germ, egg yolks, liver, green leafy vegetables, and legumes.

Functions: Choline works with inositol as a part of lecithin, important for the digestion, absorption, and transport of fats and fat-soluble vitamins (A, D, E, and K). Choline is also necessary for the production of DNA and RNA. Helps to regulate liver and gall bladder function, and can prevent gallstones. Useful in the treatment of nephritis, high blood pressure, atherosclerosis, and glaucoma.

Deficiency: May result in high blood pressure, cirrhosis and fatty degeneration of the liver, high cholesterol level, atherosclerosis, and hardening of arteries.

RDA: Not yet established. Many authorities recommend 500 to 1,000 mg., to be taken with other B-complex vitamins.

INOSITOL (A B-complex Vitamin)

Sources: Nutritional yeast, wheat germ, lecithin, whole grains (especially oatmeal and corn), nuts, milk, blackstrap molasses, citrus fruits, and liver.

Functions: Vital for hair growth and healthy heart muscle. Can help reduce or prevent hair loss, high blood cholesterol, obesity, and schizophrenia (as part of brain cell nutrition).

Deficiency: May result in hair loss, constipation, eczema, eye disorders, and high blood cholesterol.

RDA: Not yet established. Many authorities recommend 500 to 1,000 mg., to be taken with choline and other B-complex vitamins.

FOLIC ACID (Vitamin B_9)

Sources: Dark green leafy vegetables, broccoli, asparagus, lima beans, Irish potatoes, lettuce, nutritional yeast, nuts, mushrooms, wheat germ, and liver.

Functions: Works with vitamin B_{12} in the formation of red blood cells. Necessary for cellular growth and division and for the synthesis of DNA and RNA. Important for protein metabolism and the production of antibodies that prevent and heal infections. Folic acid may be useful in the prevention and treatment of circulation problems, diarrhea, dropsy, stomach ulcers, menstrual troubles, anemia, radiation injuries and burns, and sprue (a tropical nutritional deficiency disease whose symptoms include anemia and chronic diarrhea).

Deficiency: May result in anemia, skin trouble, loss of

hair, poor circulation, grey-brown skin pigmentation, fatigue, depression, loss of libido in males, reproductive disorders such as miscarriages, and difficulties in childbirth.

RDA: Not yet established. MDR is 0.4 mg., to be taken with other B-complex vitamins.

PABA (Vitamin B_x or Para-aminobenzoic Acid)

Sources: Nutritional yeast, whole grains, milk, eggs, yogurt, wheat germ, blackstrap molasses, and liver. Also produced by symbiotic bacteria in healthy intestines.

Functions: Helps prevent premature aging of skin and hair. Soothes the pain of burns, and can be used in the treatment and prevention of sunburns. Helpful also in treating skin disorders such as eczema and lupus erythematosus.

Deficiency: May result in chronic fatigue, eczema, anemia, prematurely gray hair and wrinkled skin, reproductive difficulties, and loss of libido in males.

RDA: Not yet established. Available only by prescription in dosages greater than 30 mg. Should be taken with other B-complex vitamins.

BIOTIN (Vitamin H)

Sources: Nutritional yeast (best source), unpolished rice, soya beans, liver, and kidneys. Produced in healthy intestines by symbiotic bacteria.

Functions: Involved in protein and fat metabolism and in growth and maintenance of healthy hair.

Deficiency: May result in eczema, seborrhea, hair loss, dandruff, skin disorders, lung infections, anemia, loss of appetite, chronic fatigue, confusion, depression, and hallucinations.

RDA: Not yet established. MDR is 150 to 300 mcg.

VITAMIN B_{12} (Cobalamin)

Sources: Milk, eggs, aged cheese, liver, nutritional yeast, sunflower seeds, comfrey leaves, kelp, bananas, peanuts, Concord grapes, wheat germ, and bee pollen.

Functions: Necessary for the production and regeneration of red blood cells. Plays an important part in many enzymic and metabolic processes.

Deficiency: May result in nutritional or pernicious anemia, poor appetite and growth in children, chronic fatigue, sore mouth, feelings of numbness and stiffness, mental sluggishness, and difficulty in concentrating.

RDA: 3 mcg.

VITAMIN B_{13} (Orotic Acid)

Sources: Whey portion of milk, especially soured milk, and organically-grown root vegetables.

Functions: Used in the metabolism of folic acid and vitamin B_{12}. Essential for the biosynthesis of nucleic acid and for cellular regenerative processes. Used with success in the treatment of multiple sclerosis. Also helps to prevent premature signs of aging.

Deficiency: May result in premature aging and overall degeneration, as of multiple sclerosis.

RDA: Not yet established. Available in supplement form as calcium orotate.

VITAMIN B_{15} (Pangamic Acid)

Sources: Apricot kernels, pumpkin and sesame seeds, nutritional yeast, brown rice, and other whole grains.

Functions: Increases tolerance to hypoxia (insufficient supply of oxygen to cells). Helps regulate fat and protein metabolism, and the oxidation of glucose. Stimulates the glandular and nervous systems and may be useful in the treatment of high blood cholesterol, poor circulation, and premature aging. Can also protect against carbon monoxide poisoning.

Deficiency: May lead to diminished oxygen supply to cells, heart disease, and glandular and nervous disorders.

RDA: Not yet established. No known toxicity level.

VITAMIN B_{17} (Laetrile)

Sources: A concentration of 2 to 3 percent is found in the whole kernels of fruits such as apricots, apples, peaches, plums, nectarines, raspberries, cranberries, blackberries, and blueberries; also found in mung beans, lima beans, garbanzos, millet, buckwheat, and flaxseed. Also present in about 70 plants commonly used as animal fodder.

Functions: Used legally in 17 countries, not including U.S., in the control and prevention of cancer.

Deficiency: May eventually result in an increased susceptibility to cancerous malignancies.

RDA: Not yet established, as its use is currently outlawed in the U.S. Deficiency is unlikely if an abundance of whole seeds, grains, nuts, beans, and other rich laetrile sources are included in the diet.

VITAMIN C (Ascorbic Acid)

Sources: Almost all fresh, unheated fruits and vegetables, such as rose hips, citrus fruit, black currants, strawberries, apples, guavas, persimmons, potatoes, cabbage, broccoli, tomatoes, turnip greens, and red and green bell peppers.

Functions: Essential for the maintenance of collagen, a protein used in the formation of connective tissues in skin, ligaments, and bones. Necessary for the construction of scar tissue—a form of connective tissue—over wounds and burns. Also important for the formation of red blood cells and prevention of hemorrhaging. Helps protect the body against allergy-producing substances and bacterial infection; also protects against bodily stress from toxic chemicals in the environment, or from drugs or snakebite.

Deficiency: May result in tooth decay, soft gums (pyorrhea), skin disorders, weak capillaries, collagen breakdown, anemia, premature aging, thyroid troubles, increased susceptibility to infections and to the toxic effects of drugs and environmental poisons. May eventually lead to scurvy.

RDA: 45 mg.

VITAMIN D

Sources: Fish liver oils, egg yolks, milk, butter, sprouted seeds, mushrooms, sunflower seeds, and exposure to sunshine.

Functions: Aids in the absorption of calcium, phosphorus, and other minerals. Necessary for the proper function of the thyroid and parathyroid glands. Essential to the proper development of teeth and bones in growing children. Most effective when taken with vitamin A.

Deficiency: May result in tooth decay, rickets, pyorrhea, osteomalacia, osteoporosis, retarded growth and poor bone formation in children, muscular weakness, fatigue, poor assimilation of minerals, and premature signs of
aging.

RDA: 400 International Units. Can be toxic if used excessively.

VITAMIN E (Tocopherol)

Sources: Cold-pressed, unrefined vegetable oils, especially wheat germ and soya bean oils; raw or sprouted seeds, nuts, and grains; fresh wheat germ (less than 1 week old); green leafy vegetables; and eggs.

Functions: Helps improve circulation, respiration, and fertility. Helps prevent the formation of scar tissue in burns and sores. Also protects against thrombosis, heart disease, asthma, phlebitis, arthritis, angina pectoris, emphysema, leg ulcers, varicose veins, and premature aging. Essential for the healthy function of reproductive organs. Has been used successfully in the treatment of burns and in the prevention and treatment of reproductive
disorders, infertility, miscarriages, stillbirths, and menopausal and menstrual disorders.

Deficiency: May result in coronary problems, pulmonary embolism, strokes, and heart disease. May lead to sexual impotency in males. Prolonged deficiency may cause spontaneous abortions, sterility, muscular disorders, and increased fragility of red blood cells.

RDA: 15 International Units.

BIOFLAVONOIDS (part of the C-complex or Vitamin "P")

Sources: Most fresh, unheated fruits and vegetables; buckwheat; citrus fruits, particularly the pulp; and red and green bell peppers.

Functions: Essential to healthy capillaries and capillary walls. Helps prevent capillary hemorrhaging, and may help prevent strokes. Helpful in the treatment of hypertension, respiratory infections, hemorrhoids, varicose veins, bleeding gums, eczema, psoriasis, cirrhosis of the liver, retinal hemorrhages, radiation sickness, coronary thrombosis, and arteriosclerosis.

Deficiency: May result in capillary weakness; purplish or blue spots from broken capillaries; decreased effectiveness of vitamin C; decreased resistance.

RDA: Not yet established.

VITAMIN F (Essential fatty acids)

Sources: Unsaturated fatty acids are found in cold-pressed unrefined vegetable oils, especially soya bean, corn, flaxseed, safflower, and sunflower oils. Saturated fatty acids are found in milk, butter, cheese, and meat drippings.

Functions: May be helpful in lowering blood cholesterol in arteriosclerosis and in the prevention of heart disease. Important to the normal function of glands, especially the adrenals; essential for healthy skin and mucous membranes. Promotes normal growth and metabolic processes and aids in cellular absorption of calcium and magnesium. Can promote resistance to radiation poisoning.

Deficiency: May result in skin disorders, such as eczema, acne, and dry skin. May also cause the formation of gallstones. Can lead to hair loss, impaired growth, reproductive malfunctions, kidney disorders, prostate problems, and menstrual troubles.

RDA: Not yet established. Recommended by many authorities: no less than 1 percent of total caloric intake.

VITAMIN K (Menadione)

Sources: Kelp, alfalfa and other green plants, soya bean oil, egg yolks, milk, and liver. Also manufactured by the bacteria in healthy intestines.

Functions: Necessary for the production of prothrombin (essential to the normal clotting of blood). Important for the proper function of the liver; promotes vitality and longevity.

Deficiency: May prevent normal clotting of blood and result in hemorrhaging of any part of the body (as in nosebleeds or bleeding ulcers). May lead to lowered vitality, and premature signs of aging.

RDA: Not yet established.

VITAMIN T ("Sesame seed factor")

Sources: Sesame seeds, tahini, sesame butter, egg yolks, and some vegetable oils.

Functions: Used in the formation of blood platelets. Can help correct nutritional anemia and hemophilia. May help improve fading memory.

Deficiency: May result in poor growth and regeneration of injured or diseased tissues.

RDA: Not yet established.

VITAMIN U ("Cabbage factor")

Sources: Fresh, unheated cabbage or cabbage juice, and homemade sauerkraut.

Functions: Aids in the reconstruction of tissues afflicted by ulcers.

RDA: Not yet established.

Minerals

CALCIUM (Ca)

Sources: Sesame seeds, kelp, sunflower seeds, green leafy vegetables, nuts, millet, milk, and cheese.

Functions: Helps build bones and teeth; aids in muscle contraction and in maintaining normal heart function; normalizes metabolism.

Deficiency: May result in porous and fragile bones (osteomalasia and osteoporosis), retarded bone and tooth development, nervousness, and muscle irritability.

RDA: 800 mg.

CHLORINE (Cl)

Sources: Kelp, sea vegetables, watercress, tomatoes, avocados, chard, cabbage, endives, turnips, celery, cucumbers, asparagus, and pineapples.

Functions: Essential for the production of hydrochloric acid in the stomach. Needed in protein digestion and mineral assimilation. Aids liver in its detoxifying activity, sustains normal heart activity, and helps maintain proper acid-alkaline balance.

Deficiency: Disturbed digestion and derangement of fluid levels in the body.

RDA: 500 mg.

COPPER (Cu)

Sources: Almonds (in fact, most nuts), beans, peas, green leafy vegetables, and prunes.

Functions: Necessary for production of RNA. Aids in protein metabolism and in development of bones, brain cells, nerves, and connective tissues. Helps retain the natural color of the hair. Necessary for absorption of iron.

Deficiency: Retarded hemoglobin production, anemia, loss of hair, disturbed digestion, defective respiration, and general debility.

RDA: 2 mg.

IODINE (I)

Sources: Sea kelp, dulse, seaweed, Swiss chard, turnip greens, watermelon, pineapples, spinach, asparagus, kale, garlic, watercress, pears, artichokes, citrus fruits, and egg yolks.

Functions: Plays an essential role in the formation of thyroxin, the thyroid hormone which helps regulate physical and mental activity. Aids oxidation of fats and proteins; stimulates circulation.

Deficiency: Goiter, enlarged thyroid gland, susceptibility to infection, reduced and depressed physical and mental activity, anemia, a tendency toward obesity, high blood cholesterol, heart disease, and often thyroid cancer.

RDA: 150 mcg.

IRON (Fe)

Sources: Kelp, dulse, sea vegetables, apricots, peaches, bananas, prunes, raisins, green leafy vegetables, beets, nutritional yeast, alfalfa, all seeds, and egg yolks.

Functions: Aids in the formation of hemoglobin, which carries the oxygen from the lungs to every cell of the body, resulting in a higher resistance to stress and disease.

Deficiency: Iron deficiency anemia, lowered resistance to disease, persistent headaches, and shortness of breath while exercising. Some nutritionists suggest a lowered sexual interest.

RDA: Males 10 mg.; females 18 mg.

MAGNESIUM (Mg)

Sources: Nuts (especially almonds), soya beans, dried fruits, green leafy vegetables, figs, bananas, apples, lemons, peaches, sunflower and sesame seeds, kelp, and whole grains.

Functions: Activates enzymes in carbohydrate metabolism; aids in the utilization of vitamins B and E, fats, and calcium and other minerals. Essential for healthy muscle tone and bones, and for efficient synthesis of proteins. Conditions liver and glands; aids in the regulation of acid-alkaline balance and lecithin production. Can help in combating cholesterol build-up. A natural tranquilizer.

Deficiency: Muscular irritability, heart beat acceleration, convulsion, kidney stone formation. Can contribute to premature aging.

RDA: 350 mg.

MANGANESE (Mn)

Sources: Chives, parsley, celery, cucumbers, carrots, beets, green leafy vegetables, oranges, grapefruits, apricots, outer coating of nuts and grains, peas, wheat germ, kelp, and egg yolks.

Functions: Helps in fat digestion and utilization when combined with chlorine. Aids in brain and nerve nourishment and assists in the coordinative action between brain, nerves, and muscles. Helps in normal reproduction and in the function of mammary glands.

Deficiency: Possible sterility, growth retardation, digestive problems (excessive gas), abnormal bone development, and respiratory disorders.

RDA: Not yet established.

PHOSPHORUS (P)

Sources: Dark green leafy vegetables, whole grains, seeds, nuts, legumes, dried fruits, corn, egg yolks, and dairy products.

Functions: Works in concert with calcium to aid in the metabolism of fat and carbohydrates. Needed for healthy bones and teeth; essential for maintaining an appropriate acid-alkaline balance.

Deficiency: Poor mineralization of bones, poor growth, deficient nerve and brain function, and general weakness.

RDA: 800 mg. Deficiency is rare.

POTASSIUM (K)

Sources: Seaweed, dulse, legumes, dried fruits, all vegetables (but especially green leafy ones), whole grains, nuts, sunflower seeds, bananas, potatoes, and potato skins.

Functions: Essential in maintaining proper acid-alkaline balance in blood and tissues, and in maintaining intercellular fluid balance. Aids in formation of glycogen from glucose, fats from glycogen, and proteins from peptones and proteoses. Helps kidneys in detoxification of blood. Stimulates endocrine hormone production. Involved in proper function of the nervous system.

Deficiency: Excessive accumulation of sodium (salt) in tissues resulting in edema (sodium poisoning), high blood pressure, and possible heart failure. Interferes with digestion resulting in constipation, nervous disorders, fatigue, inadequate muscle control, and low blood sugar (hypoglycemia).

RDA: Not yet established; dietary need equivalent to that of sodium.

SELENIUM (Se)

Sources: Sea water, kelp, whole grains, and most vegetables.

Functions: Has an anti-oxidant effect similar to vitamin E. Biological activity closely related to that of vitamin E, having a "sparing" effect on the body's use of that vitamin. Also helps in the rejuvenation of the liver and prevention of hemoglobin damage from oxidation. Counteracts and protects the body from toxin damage by mercury poisoning.

Deficiency: Weakened muscles, premature aging, and liver function disruption and eventual damage.

RDA: Not yet established; toxic in overdosage.

SILICON (Si)

Sources: Kelp, steel-cut oats, green leafy vegetables, dandelion greens, strawberries, cucumbers, grapes, beets, onions, nuts, and sunflower seeds.

Functions: Builds strong bones; maintains normal growth of hair, nails, and teeth. Protective agent against many respiratory diseases, irritation to the mucous membranes, and skin disorders.

Deficiency: General weakness, reduced resistance to infectious diseases, wrinkles, soft brittle nails, thinning or loss of hair, poor bone development, insomnia, and osteoporosis.

RDA: Not yet established.

SODIUM (Na)

Sources: Kelp, sea salt, beet greens, celery, kale, carrots, raisins, radishes, dried fruits, romaine lettuce, watermelon, and asparagus.

Functions: Important in hydrochloric acid production in the stomach; involved in many glandular secretions. Helps to control and maintain cellular osmotic pressure and water balance. Works with potassium and chlorine.

Deficiency: Deficiency, resulting in chronic diarrhea, is rare. Overconsumption, not deficiency, is the problem: water retention, high blood pressure, stomach ulcers, hardening of the arteries, and heart disease.

RDA: 200–600 mg. from whole foods, not from a salt shaker.

SULFUR (S)

Sources: Onions, radishes, garlic, watercress, soya beans, turnips, celery, stringbeans, kelp, raspberries, and lettuce.

Functions: Helps to maintain healthy hair, skin, and nails. Serves as an essential oxidizing agent in hemoglobin. Aids digestion and elimination.

Deficiency: Poor growth of nails and hair; skin defects such as eczema, dermatitis, rashes, and blemishes.

RDA: Not yet established.

ZINC (Zn)

Sources: Wheat germ, wheat bran, unhulled sesame seeds, pumpkin and sunflower seeds, nutritional yeast, egg yolks, onions, green leafy vegetables, and sprouted seeds.

Functions: Aids in healing of wounds and burns. Participates in the transfer of carbon dioxide from tissues to lungs. Essential for the formation of RNA and DNA. Plays an active role in the synthesis of body protein.

Deficiency: Growth retardation, birth defects, underdeveloped gonads, prostate enlargement and dysfunction, and loss of fertility. Slowed healing of wounds, lowered resistance to infections, hair loss, and dandruff.

RDA: 15 mg.

Cobalt (Co) is a component of vitamin B_{12}; found in all green vegetables, it aids in the assimilation and synthesis of vitamin B_{12}.

Molybdenum (Mo) is involved with proper carbohydrate metabolism. It is an integral part of certain enzymes involved in the oxidation process. Whole grains and legumes are good sources.

Lithium (Li) is involved in sodium metabolism and transportation and is essential in the proper functioning of the autonomic nervous system. Sources include kelp, sea water, and natural lithium-rich mineral spring water.

Trace minerals such as *nickel, tin, strontium,* and *vanadium,* to name a few, are found in the body in minute form. Although we cannot elaborate here on the sources, functions, and deficiency symptoms for all the trace minerals, a sufficient intake of raw foods, seeds, wheat germ, sea vegetables, vegetable oils, and nuts will provide nutritional protection from deficiency.

Proteins

Naturopathic physicians and holistic doctors who are more in tune with the human body than with test tubes suggest a daily protein intake of 28 to 40 grams. This is closer to my sentiments and my experience than the RDA (Recommended Dietary Allowances) shown here, as adapted from the test tube derived information of the National Academy of Sciences. I include this chart not to show how much protein you supposedly need daily (a figure the test tubers are constantly revising downward anyway), but to suggest the relationship of protein need at various ages.

Sex and Age in Years		*Weight in Pounds*	*Height in Inches*	*Calories*	*Proteins in grams*
Men	11–14	97	63	2800	44
	15–18	134	69	3000	54
	19–22	147	69	3000	54
	23–50	154	69	2700	56
	51+	154	69	2400	56
Women	11–14	97	62	2400	44
	15–18	119	65	2100	48
	19–22	128	65	2100	46
	23–50	128	65	2000	46
	51+	128	65	1800	46
Pregnant				+300	+30
Lactating				+500	+20

Adapted from Recommended Daily Dietary Allowances, Food and Nutrition Board, National Academy of Sciences—National Research Council, revised 1974.

I've included this chart, adapted from material in Carqués *Rational Diet,* to show which nuts, legumes, and grains are highest in protein.

Approximate amount of food to supply 2 oz. (56 grams) of usable protein.

Shelled Nuts	*Amount Used*
Pignolias	6 oz.
Black walnuts	7 oz.
Butter nuts	7 oz.
Peanuts	7 oz.
Almond butter	8 oz.
Pistachio nuts	9 oz.
Almonds	9 oz.
Beechnuts	10 oz.
Brazil nuts	11 oz.
English walnuts	11 oz.
Filberts	12½ oz.
Pinons	14 oz.
Pecans	16 oz.
Chestnuts	20 oz.
Coconut, dried	30 oz.

Legumes and grains	*Amount Used*
Soya beans, dried	6 oz.
Beans, dried	8 oz.
Lentils, dried	8 oz.
Peas, dried	9 oz.
Lima beans, dried	10 oz.
Green peas	30 oz.
Whole wheat	14 oz.
Rye	17 oz.
Barley	18 oz.
Oats	19 oz.
Corn	20 oz.
Millet	21 oz.
Rice	25 oz.
Whole wheat bread	20 oz.
Rye bread	21 oz.
White bread	21 oz.

Appendix II

The Laboratory's Promise: Bio-Synthetic Supplements

"Every cell of the body is served by the blood. A balanced bloodstream is the answer to natural health."
—V.E. Irons

Bio-Synthetic Supplements

For centuries, humankind has been content to savor the delights of Nature's Garden, and Nature's Garden has easily provided sufficient and healthful sustenance for pastoral man. But today, a cuisine has evolved of synthetic, overly-processed, embalmed foods hurriedly eaten by those who must daily deal with urban stress and competition seasoned with civilization's pollution.

As we become increasingly aware of how far we have come from the simple natural life of long ago, it is easy to see Nature as all good and science as all bad. Chemists, for example, are raged at as tools of the food conglomerates at best and blundering idiots and profiteers at worst. I do not believe this. There are a number of dedicated biochemists and nutritional researchers who are capable of duplicating many of Nature's wonders. We of the New Age must cooperate, not struggle, with Nature.

Vitamin and mineral supplements are partly or wholly composed of synthesized elements not occurring spontaneously in Nature. Combining these bio-synthethic elements with natural foods can insure optimal health and well-being. Please remember, these are supplements, not substitutes.

Bio-synthetic supplements, like foods, require careful and conscious combination for best assimilation by the body. With the cost of commercial supplements so high, knowledge of proper combinations is not only essential to health, but economical as well.

In choosing vitamin supplements, look for the following characteristics:

1) Multivitamin
2) Time release
3) Free from artificial flavors, colors, or binders
4) Free from carbohydrates
5) Cold processed
6) Obtained from natural rather than synthetic sources

In addition, vitamin E should contain all of the natural tocopherols, and vitamin C should be made from acerola or rose hips and contain all of the bioflavonoids. When combining vitamins and minerals, remember:

1) Vitamin A combines well with natural calcium and magnesium; this is especially effective when taken before breakfast.
2) The B vitamins combine well with natural chelated

iron and zinc, and all trace minerals. The B vitamins, especially vitamin B_{12}, combine poorly with vitamin C.

3) Vitamin C combines well with vitamins A and E.

4) Vitamin C supplementary forms are best in time release or chewable form.

5) Vitamin E combines well with A, but it is not advisable to combine E with iron unless the iron is chelated. Iron without copper is harmful to the body.

If mineral supplements are used, be sure that they are chelated, as chelated minerals are nearly one hundred percent assimilable by the body; inorganic mineral compounds seldom contribute to health and can be toxic.

Protein supplements should be free from sugar or artificial sweeteners. If you feel the need for a sweet protein supplement, use the kind that contains fructose, a fruit sugar.

Appendix III

The Cleansing Diet

The quality of our blood is contingent upon the nutritional elements found in the foods we eat. The blood nourishes the cells, replaces worn-out parts, and carries away waste products. When the nutritionally derived materials in the blood are not of the quality or in the quantity necessary, the organs or glands may malfunction; the components necessary for resistance to disease are missing.

The body must have the capacity to maintain health. Internal pollution is destructive. The extravaganza of modern cookery, the convenience of processed and embalmed foods, and our modern eating habits have distorted the natural digestive processes, resulting in disease due to malabsorption and inferior nutrition.

The secret lies in the intestines. In the villi of the small intestines the body absorbs proteins, fats, carbohydrates, and vitamins. In the large intestine, minerals, water, and any remaining nutrients are absorbed. What remains after this is unusable to the body, and should be eliminated as soon as possible. When waste matter remains too long in the intestine, so much water is absorbed from it that the matter becomes dry, hard, and increasingly toxic. The result is constipation and other problems related to the inability to eliminate waste and toxic matter. Unless we restore and maintain intestinal integrity we may fall victim to poor health and disease. Cleansing programs are the first step in the process of building and maintaining healthy blood.

Your physician should be educated in how to restore intestinal health through a program of internal cleansing. Synthetic medications and drugs interfere with the body's natural functions and contribute to the malabsorption syndrome. Only nature cures and heals; your doctor must be a humble assistant.

I have worked with many of the cleansing and absorbing programs. Among the most effective ones I'm familiar with are those described in Dr. Stone's *Purifying Diet,* Dr. Shelton's *Fasting Can Save Your Life,* Dr. Airola's *How to Keep Slim, Healthy, and Young With Juice Fasting,* and V.E. Irons' *Seven Day Cleansing Program.*
I recommend these programs to you, and hope you will examine all of them carefully before beginning any of them. Check your local health food store for books by the authors I've mentioned, or write to the authors directly.

Fasting is of superior effectiveness in restoring the body's powers of absorption. With V.E. Irons' Cleansing Program, particularly, the results are immediate and reinforcing. This is not to discredit any of the other programs; each has its own advantages. I have a great deal of respect and admiration for all of the authors mentioned, especially in their dedication to scientific truth. But I am particularly impressed with the Irons' program, and am grateful to Mr. Irons for permission to present his program, as I have used it, here. I'd suggest that you write to Mr. Irons for complete information.

V.E. Irons' Seven Day Cleansing Program*

The night before beginning the program, take one or two of the herb tablets from the Cleanser can. Then, each day for seven full days, eat nothing other than as specified here. Take the Cleansing Combination five times a day, every three hours; drink plenty of water, in addition to what is specified, especially whenever you feel hungry. Plenty of water is essential to the Program.

The Cleansing Combination is prepared in a 1 pint glass jar with a tight-fitting lid. Pour into the jar about one inch of your choice of apple, pineapple, orange, or grape juice (fresh, frozen concentrate, or canned). The juice prevents too quick jelling of the cleanser and adds flavor. Add at least ten ounces of water, one tablespoon of Bentonite (#19), and one heaping teaspoon of the Cleanser (#16) last of all, to prevent thickening. Cover and shake jar vigorously for about fifteen seconds. Drink rapidly.

One and a half hours after taking the Cleansing Combination, that is, midway between doses, take six tablets of your choice of Vit-ra-tox #21 or #22 (I recommend #22 since it contains less matter to be digested and one aim of this program is to give your system a rest.)

This regimen also includes, for best results, strong black coffee enemas every night for the seven days of the Program. Make two quarts of coffee each time, using 8 tablespoons of regular ground coffee. Coffee in enemas or colonics stimulates peristaltic movement. Be sure to use lukewarm water; do not place the water bag more than two feet above the rectum. Lie on your side on the bathroom floor or in the bathtub and allow only one-half cup to enter at a time. Before any pressure is felt, stop and massage the lower abdomen thoroughly for several minutes. Continue to add small amounts of water, pausing frequently so that no pressure is created. Continue until solid matter appears.

After the seventh day, take the Cleansing Combination (juice, water, #16, #19) morning and evening only until two natural bowel movements occur. Continue using the #21 tablets and #22 tablets for two months (take four of the #21, four times a day, and 5 of the #22, 4 times a day), then reduce to the amount indicated on the label. Resume normal eating but eliminate from your diet anything made with bleached or refined flours or sugars. Use unrefined whole grain products and honey, raw sugar, or molasses. Eat a raw vegetable salad every day, and one lightly cooked leafy vegetable. Eat raw fresh fruits daily; eat melon often. Remember to cook all your foods (meats too, if you are eating meats) *very* briefly. See that half of your food intake is uncooked; try to eat raw fresh food at every meal. Drink plenty of water between meals, and get lots of exercise. Walk as much as possible.

* Materials needed for the Cleansing Program are available from V.E. Irons, Inc., Natick, Massachusetts 01760, or from a physician who employs the program.

Index